Stately **Service**

# Stately Service

## The changing scene below stairs

Published by VisitBritain Publishing in association with the Historic Houses Association

VisitBritain Publishing
Thames Tower, Blacks Road, London W6 9EL

First published 2007

© British Tourist Authority (trading as VisitBritain) with Susanna Geoghegan Gift Publishing Consultancy 2007

ISBN 978-0-7095-8404-9
Product code: TNSTSER

A CIP catalogue record for this book is available from the British Library.

All rights reserved. No part of this publication may be reproduced, stored in a retrieval system, or transmitted in any form or by any means, electronic, mechanical, photocopying, recording, or otherwise, without the prior written permission of VisitBritain and copyright owners.

The information contained in this publication has been published in good faith on the basis of information submitted to VisitBritain and is believed to be correct at time of going to press. Nevertheless, VisitBritain regrets that it cannot guarantee complete accuracy and all liability for loss, disappointment, negligence or other damages caused by reliance on the information contained in this publication, is hereby excluded.

Designed and produced for VisitBritain Publishing by Susanna Geoghegan Gift Publishing Consultancy
Printed in China

# Contents

# Foreword

*Stately Service* forms part of the 'Then and Now' series which has been published in association with the Historic Houses Association (HHA).

As its title suggests, the series looks at the life and work of Britain's historic houses today – attracting, as they do, more than 15 million visitors a year, providing employment for upwards of 10,000 people (who annually earn in excess of £85 million) and contributing an estimated £1.6–£2 billion each year to the rural economy – and compares and contrasts this with times past, when these houses and their estates were largely the exclusive preserve of their owners and their guests.

It is a fascinating and inspiring subject, which has been made all the more illuminating thanks to the very considerable help of a large number of people: owners who have set aside time in busy schedules to give interviews and answer questions, administrators who have coordinated research, archivists who have made available much valuable material from past and present, members of staff who have broken off what they were doing to chat freely about their work (which in a number of cases spans several decades at the same property).

We extend our very grateful thanks to them all, in particular the following, who have been closely involved with the series throughout its evolution:

At the HHA itself, Peter Sinclair and Fiona Attenborough.

At Ballindalloch Castle, Mrs Clare Macpherson-Grant Russell Laird of Ballindalloch, her husband Oliver Russell and Fenella Corr.

At Chatsworth, the Duke of Devonshire, Simon Seligman, Charles Noble, Stuart Band, Andrew Peppitt, Diana Naylor and Glyn Motley.

At Eastnor Castle, James Hervey-Bathurst and Simon Foster.

At Fonmon Castle, Sir Brooke Boothby.

At Loseley Park, Michael More-Molyneux, Major James More-Molyneux, Nichola Cheriton-Sutton and Isabel Sullivan (who looks after the Loseley archives at Surrey History Centre).

At Newby Hall, Richard Compton, Robin Compton and Stuart Gill.

At Powderham Castle, the Earl and Countess of Devon, Lady Katherine Watney, Clare Crawshaw, Felicity Harper, Ginny Bowman and Christine Manning.

At Ripley Castle, Sir Thomas Ingilby and Alison Crawford.

In addition we would like to thank three of the above as authors who have kindly permitted us to quote from their work. They, and their books, are: Sir Thomas Ingilby, *Yorkshire's Great Houses* (Dalesman Publishing 2005); James More-Molyneux, *The Loseley Challenge* (Hodder & Stoughton 1995); Clare Macpherson-Grant Russell, *"I Love Food"* (Heritage House Group Ltd 2006).

# Introduction

According to *The Servant's Practical Guide* of 1880 'the largest establishments' usually employed upwards of thirty household servants, who were assigned carefully prescribed duties, which ensured a ready supply of conveniences and comforts for the owning family and their guests. In contrast servants often found themselves sharing dormitories with other servants, completing much of the day-to-day housekeeping before the family surfaced, eating and socialising in the servants' hall and having little free time of their own.

A century on, service as it was perceived in its Victorian and Edwardian heyday, when one in three girls between the ages of fifteen and twenty were employed as servants, has disappeared. Technology has taken over many of the tasks that they once performed by hand. Areas of the house behind the scenes, which were once essential in its smooth running have been made redundant by improved transport and the general march of time. Even the largest historic houses employ just a small team of staff, who now live in estate cottages or comfortable flats, and enjoy a degree of independence that would have been unimaginable to their predecessors.

While the nature of 'service' for those employed to look after owners and their guests may have changed significantly, the tradition of hospitality and entertainment in many historic houses has advanced to a new level. Today these magnificent homes and their gardens host lavish lunches, dinners, product launches, corporate banquets and sumptuous weddings – a great many of which are still masterminded by the owners and the professional events organisers and caterers who work with them.

The nature of service in a great house may have changed, but in terms of quality and expertise, not to mention setting, it's very much a case of business as usual.

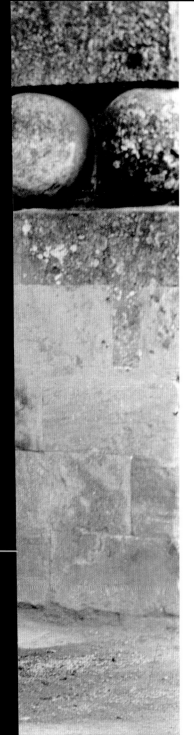

# From Livery
## to Housecoat

A century ago those employed in 'service' were regulated by a strict hierarchy. The work they did carried clear demarcations, as did their pay and in many cases even the clothes they wore to perform their duties.

Vestiges of this way of life survived well into the twentieth century. When Michael More-Molyneux's grandfather lived in his family's magnificent Elizabethan home, Loseley Park near Guildford, his life was made easier by the attentions of a butler, an under-butler, a cook and a housekeeper – and by the standards of many of his peers this was a very modest household.

When his son, Major James More-Molyneux, and his wife Sue took on the daunting responsibility of bringing the house and estate back from the brink after the Second World War, they were helped by a just a couple of staff: one cooked, the other cleaned. Today, Loseley is looked after by Michael's wife Sarah, aided by a lady who takes care of the ironing and two stalwart ladies who clean for three mornings a week, one of whom has been part of the Loseley team for over thirty years and the other for more

**Lodge Porter, resplendent in full livery, at the gate of Blenheim Palace accompanied by Blenheim spaniels.**

11

than twenty years – and theirs is a familiar pattern found in a great many historic houses up and down the country.

Modern, labour-saving technology has played its part in removing much of the drudgery and back-breaking tedium of service in both the house and grounds, which characterised the days when virtually everything in the house had to be done by hand. But those changes took centuries to evolve; only seventy years ago there were more working women employed in service in Britain than in any other occupation. This followed a tradition that reached back hundreds of years as the records of many stately homes testify.

These days the cleaning of Powderham Castle, the historic family home of the Earls of Devon, comes under the care of Christine Manning and Sue Underhill, who is also manageress of the Castle's Courtyard Tea Rooms. 'It's not to the same standard as it was in the old days,' Christine acknowledges, 'because there isn't the time to do it.' Every morning she makes a note of what needs attention the following day. 'You can't do one

Before mechanisation, when labour was plentiful, perfectly manicured lawns required more than simple mowing.

13

room at a time,' she explains. 'You have to do all the rooms, because they're all open to the public, apart from the ones on this [the family's private] side.' And the cleaning has to take place before the first tour parties enter at 10.30, after which time Christine and her Henry vacuum cleaner dodge from one room to another dusting and disappearing as they go. Apart from seeing her polishing the large brass dolphins on the front door, or watering the flowers in the Terrace Entrance, visitors to Powderham Castle seldom catch sight of the dedicated duo who keep the rooms pristine.

In many respects Christine Manning reflects a widespread tradition of working in, and a close attachment to, historic houses that frequently spans several generations. Christine was born on the Powderham Estate, where most of her family have been employed. Her grandfather was a woodman. Her uncle Arthur was the house carpenter; a role that then passed to Christine's father, George, and is now the responsibility of her brother, Gerald Hitchcock. The term house carpenter belies the extensive knowledge and

expertise that position called for in days gone by and continues to demand even in an age of specialist furniture restorers. From repairing antique clocks, to mending period furniture, the house carpenter combines the roles of cabinet-maker, handyman and horologist. Gerald's father was in the habit of discreetly writing his initials on the back of items he repaired and, a generation later, Gerald is coming across those repairs in the course of his own work, adding his own initials beside his father's when he finishes a job. Of course the house carpenter's work is not restricted to repairs; when Lord and Lady Devon needed a table to replace a piece of furniture in the state dining-room, it was Gerald Hitchcock who made one from oak grown on the estate.

At the beginning of her more than forty years' employment at Powderham, Christine Manning worked with the horses and the herd of South Devon cattle. Married in 1950, she was still riding when she was six months pregnant and the then Lady Devon suggested it might be a good idea if she took things a little easier and worked inside the house. 'It was different, then,' Christine remembers. 'It was harder – black-leading the fireplaces. These days you use a hoover on all the edges to remove all the dust. The black lead comes in tubes and you put it on with one brush, really rubbing it in, like brushing your shoes. Then you polish it off afterwards with another brush.

'The first time I was asked to do it, nearly fifty years ago now, by a lovely woman: Alice Goodwin, who was here for thirty-three years. She asked me if I would do the fireplace [in the dining-hall] and when we all met together to have a cup of tea mid-morning, they all burst out laughing when I walked in. I had black spots all over me. I'd never done it before and I was covered in black lead. It's awful stuff to get off, but the fireplaces do look nice when they're done.'

Cleaning that fireplace took the best part of two hours. For Christine's predecessors and their peers in centuries past, this represented just a part of the daily toil that shaped their lives, not only at Powderham Castle, but in every household where open fires were burned, and dust and grime gathered.

**The grind and grime of black-leading the household's fireplaces was a feature of daily life for every housemaid.**

The archives at Powderham Castle include lists of servants in the household of Sir William Courtenay. One of these, drawn up on Lady Day 1748, provides a fascinating illustration of the staffing levels, rates of pay and tasks undertaken by servants in mid-eighteenth-century houses such as Powderham.

There were seventy-seven domestic servants listed. They ranged in hierarchy from William Chapple, the House Steward, who received an annual wage of £50 (plus 'produce' from leases on estate lands at Honiton, and a surveyor's fee), to the housemaids, laundry maids, kitchen maids and dairy maids, who were each paid three pounds a year. Miss Courtenay's Nurse's assistant, Sarah Tamlin, received two pounds ten shillings a year, plus a gown, and the pots-man, Roger Sparke, received 'diet and clothes only'.

Moving up the pay scale, Charity Flood (chamber maid) was paid four pounds a year. The hog-man, Sam Bennett, received four guineas; the gamekeeper and wonderfully named 'Capt' Eyles Pierce was paid five pounds a year, as were the under groom and the helpers 'in coach & stable'.

Sir William's postilions were on an annual salary of six pounds a year, his valet and footmen on seven, like the groom, the under butler and the park keeper; the castle butcher topped them by an extra ten shillings year. Breaking into double figures, the coachman and 'surveyor of timber & repairs' were paid ten pounds a year; Morgan Tate, the 'menagery man' was also on an annual wage of ten pounds, but his remuneration was augmented by a 'suit of green & black coat'.

Servants in the higher pay scales included Sir William's 'yachtsmen', who received fifteen pounds twelve shillings. (Captain Peter Wills, Master of The Yacht, was the second highest paid member of Sir William Courtenay's staff with an annual salary of thirty pounds.)

Among female servants, Mrs Anne Montefore ('My Lady's Woman': ten pounds a year), Mrs Grace Hill (the housekeeper: fourteen pounds a year) and Miss Courtenay's Nurse (Mrs Tarrant: fifteen pounds a year) were the highest paid.

The two upholsterers were paid fifteen pounds a year. The butler at Powderham Castle, Francis Henshaw, received a salary of sixteen pounds a year. But his salary was outstripped by those paid to the gardener, under gardener, decoyman and cook who all received twenty pounds a year.

So much for Sir William Courtenay's domestic servants – his accounts also show salaries paid to thirty-five farm servants with varying skills and responsibilities. At the bottom of the pecking order on Lady Day 1748 were the plough boy, William Moor (paid two pounds fifteen shillings a year) and Elizabeth Stapeling, the laundry maid, who received five shillings more and pocketed three pounds a year. The pots-men on the farms and the helpers in the groom's stables were paid five pounds each. The salmon hutch man, the menagery woman, the helper in the coach stable, the farm carrier and the six ploughmen all earned six pounds a year. Thomas Rossiter, the maltmaker and brewer, received eight pounds. The coachmen, Humphry Spry and Michael Howe, were paid ten guineas each.

The Tamlin family at Ford were well represented in Sir William Courtenay's accounts. Sarah Bartlett (née Tamlin) was the housekeeper, for which she was paid ten pounds a year.  Elizabeth Tamlin, who worked as the dairywoman, was paid ten pounds 'on own Diet, £5 on Sir William's Diet' – the distinction being whether or not Sir William and his family were in residence.

The same arrangement applied to William Tamlin, who was paid twenty pounds a year 'on own Diet, £12 on Sir William's Diet' and to John Lamprey, the gardener at Ford who received eighteen pounds annually 'on own Diet, £5 on Sir William's Diet'.

Heading the estate staff in 1748 were the surveyor 'Mr James Garrett – Salary £21' and 'Wood Warden & Inspector Estates at Morton, Mr James Tynes – Salary £20'.

Perhaps the most startling fact among this plethora of payments and ancillary perks for well over 100 people was that Sir William's wages bill in a twelve-month period amounted to approximately £1,000.

These detailed instructions for a nineteenth-century housemaid would have struck a chord with domestic servants well into the twentieth century: 'The house maid, in a regular family, will find it necessary to rise about five o'clock, and her first business will be to open the shutters of the usual family sitting-rooms; as the breakfast-room and library, whence she clears away all the superfluous articles that may have been left there, and prepares for cleaning the stoves, fireplaces, and hearths, by rolling up the hearth rugs, carefully carrying them out to be shaken, and then laying down a piece of canvas, or coarse cloth, to keep the place clean, while she rakes out the ashes, takes them up, and brushes up the fireplaces. She then rubs the bright bars of the stoves, and the fire-irons, first with oil, and afterwards with emery-paper, No 3, or with brick dust, till clean and bright—and, finally, with scoring paper; and this should be done in the summer time, particularly when the stoves may have acquired spots for want of constant use.

'The backs and sides of the fireplaces are next to be brushed over with black-lead, and then rubbed dry and bright with a hard brush kept for the purpose.

'The fires are next lighted, and the marble hearths washed with flannel, dipped in a strong hot lather of soap and water, which must be cleaned off and wiped dry with a linen cloth; the marble chimney pieces need not be thus cleaned above once or twice a week.

'Common free-stone hearths may be scoured with soap and sand and cold water, and afterwards rubbed dry with a clean house cloth …

'On the general cleaning days also, which are usually Tuesday and Saturday, every branch of the household work must be thoroughly done, in the best manner; the rooms are then to be scoured instead of being merely wiped or swept; the carpets are to be well brushed or taken up to be beaten or shaken; the stoves and fireplaces brightened and cleaned with particular care; the marble hearths and chimney-pieces scoured; the mahogany furniture and the brass or other ornaments in the best room, and the mirrors and looking-glasses cleaned, with more than ordinary

**Below stairs the housemaid's closet formed the working hub of household cleaning.**

**Up and down the stairs from kitchen to family quarters, the servants were on the go from dawn until dusk.**

attention;—the bed furniture, window curtains and hangings well shaken, whisked and crushed: in short, the best practical methods for thoroughly cleaning the whole house, must be resorted to on that day.'

As recently as eighty years ago the housemaid's duties in a household with only a small number of staff could present a depressing challenge. A young housemaid starting work at the age of fourteen, at Ackleton Manor in Shropshire, in 1926 faced this timetable:

> **6.30 a.m.** *Draw back the curtains and open the windows in Day Nursery. Shake rug outside, clean grate, light fire, put out coal buckets. Wash floor, dust furniture and lay table for Nursery breakfast. Clean children's shoes. Repeat cleaning in Morning Room.*

> **8.00 a.m.** *Take up Nursery breakfast. Have own breakfast.*

> **8.35 a.m.** *Strip beds in Night Nursery and leave to air. Empty hot water bottles, fold night clothes and tidy room. Repeat in own room and front bedroom. Clear Nursery table and take down*

dishes. Help Nurse carry in Baby's bath. Make beds, empty slops and sweep floors in all bedrooms, while Parlour maid dusts furniture. Brush top landing and stairs, dust furniture and doors, except every other Monday when wash landing and clean stairs.

**10.15 a.m.** Wash Dining Room breakfast dishes and Nursery dishes.

The rest of the morning was given over to weekly tasks:

**Monday:** Get ready laundry, Turn out own bedroom or landing and stairs.

**Tuesday:** Turn out Dining Room or front bedroom.

**Wednesday:** Turn out Night Nursery, North Room and spare room.

**Thursday:** Turn out Day Nursery.

**Friday:** Turn out Drawing Room or Morning Room.

**Saturday:** Clean hall brasses, Turn out Servants' Hall, sweep cellar steps and outside lavatory.

**Sunday:** Change all bed linen. Give Cook a hand.

The daily chores resumed at 12.15:

**12.15 p.m.** Clean bathroom, lavatory. Lay table for Nursery lunch.

**1.00 p.m.** Take Nursery lunch and have own. Wash up in scullery. Lay Nursery tea.

**2.30 p.m.** Push second pram, except Tuesdays and Sundays when free.

**4.15 p.m.** Lay tea in Servants' Hall, clear away and wash up.

**5.00 p.m.** Bring down Nursery tea things, wash and take back.

**6.00 p.m.** Sewing and mending for Mistress, except Fridays when own mending to be done.

**7.30 p.m.** Lay table for supper in Servants' Hall.

**7.45 p.m.** Help wait at table with Parlourmaid. During dinner go upstairs and turn down beds. Wash up in pantry.

**10.00 p.m.** Bed.

Keeping a Victorian house clean became something akin to a crusade in many households.

**The daily round, the common toil.**

In the 1880s, Shirley Forster, author of *Our Homes*, exhorted her readers to take up the struggle in these bellicose terms: 'If we commence a war against dirt, we can never lay down our arms and say, "now the enemy is conquered."…Women – mistresses of households, domestic servants – are the soldiers who are deputed by society to engage in this war against dirt…As in a campaign each officer is told off to a particular duty, let each servant in a house, and each member of the family who can take a part understand clearly what is the duty for which she is responsible.'

As leader of this valiant band, the mistress, or housekeeper, was given these helpful tips in marshalling her troops: '…it will be found a good plan to write down the daily work of each servant in a little book that can hang in her cupboard, and the hours for doing it, as well as the days on which extra cleaning is required. The hours of rising, meals, dressing, shutting up, going to bed, and of all manners relating to comfort and order, should also be inscribed in the book, with existent rules, concerning 'followers', Sundays out, times for returning, the lists of silver, china, linen, pots and pans, or whatever goods are entrusted to her, the sweep's days, the dustman's days, &c., &c.'

Working in larger households, where more servants were employed, had the obvious advantage of spreading the workload. On the whole living conditions were better as well and there was a sense of camaraderie in the servants' hall. There was a rigid hierarchy here as well, however, an example of which is recorded in the memoirs of Lady Augusta Fane, who recalled how the upper servants would progress from the servants' hall to the housekeeper's parlour, 'The Room', at mealtimes:

**Dinner in the servants' hall of a large household: the butler presides, with housekeeper, ladies' maids, housemaids and footmen arranged in order of seniority.**

**Answering back was never an option.**

'This was a serious ceremony; the butler and housekeeper and lady's maid had their meat course in the "hall", the butler carving whilst the hall-boy waited. When the sweets were handed round, the upper servants rose from the table, each carrying a plate of pudding in one hand and a glass of beer in the other, and walked majestically out of the room in single file according to the rank of their master or mistress. The ladies' maids and valets were always addressed amongst themselves by the name of their employers. A well-bred but untitled girl said that her lady's maid, after having been with her several years, gave notice. Asked why, she replied that she was very happy but it hurt her feelings always to have to walk out last from the hall, so she wanted to take a situation with a titled lady or at least with an honourable.'

A similar approach to discipline prevailed in all well-regulated households and the rules codified at Clandon Park in Surrey, itemising correct behaviour in the servants' hall (and forfeits for any breaches), would have been familiar to servants in all such establishments.

# Staff Rules

1 Whoever is last at Breakfast to clear the Table and put the Copper, Horns, Salt, Pepper & in their proper places, or forfeit . . . 3d.

2 The servants' hall Cloth laid for Dinner by 1 o'Clock, and not omit laying the Salt, Pepper, and Spoons . . . 3d.

3 The Housekeeper's room Knives to Clean'd ev'ry day by the Usher of this hall. . . . 3d.

4 That if any Person be heard to Swear, or Use any Indecent language at any time when the Cloth is on the table, He is to forfeit . . . 3d.

5 Whoever leaves any thing belonging to their Dress or any Wearing Apparel out of their proper places . . . 3d.

6 That no one be suffered to Play at Cards in the Hall before six o'Clock in the Evening . . . 3d.

7 Whoever leaves any Pieces of Bread at Breakfast, Dinner, or Supper . . . 1d.

8 That if any one shall be observed cleaning livery clothes, or leather breeches, at any time of Meals; or shall leave any dirt after cleaning them at any time.. . . 3d.

9 That the Usher to have the Hall decently Swept and the dirt taken away before dinner time . . . 3d.

10 That no one shall put any kind of provisions in any Cupboard or Drawer in the Hall after their meal but shall return it from whence they had it. . . . 3d.

11 That the Table Cloth shall after all meals be folded up and put in the drawer for that purpose . . . 3d.

12 That if anyone be observ'd wiping their Knives in the table cloth at any time . . . 3d.

13 That if any stable or other servant take any plates to the stable, or be seen to set them for Dogs to eat off . . . 3d.

14 That no wearing apparel to hang in the Hall, but shall be put in the Closets for that purpose . . . 3d.

15 All stable and other servants to come to dinner with their Coats on . . . 3d.

Free time and holidays were luxuries that no one employed in service in days gone by could enjoy on anything like the scale we expect today. In 1880, *The Servants' Practical Guide* gave details of the sort of free time a servant might expect to be given, 'The general rule is, that servants should have the opportunity of attending church once every Sunday, and twice every other Sunday,

either morning, afternoon or evening, according as the work of the house is arranged between themselves and their fellow-servants, during their temporary absence. They are also allowed one afternoon a week for going out and a whole day or half a day once a month.'

But it would be wrong for one generation to look too critically at the working practices of an earlier generation without considering the social and domestic conditions at that time. William Lanceley started out working as a footboy in the 1880s before graduating to be a fully-fledged footman. At this humble level in the household his duties were largely concerned with attending to the needs of his superiors in the servants' hall. His day started at six in the morning and writing his memoirs in 1925, the memory of what he had to do was still clearly etched in his mind.

'First light the servants' hall fire, clean the young ladies' boots, the butler's, housekeeper's, cook's and ladies' maids', often twenty pairs altogether, trim the lamps (I had thirty-five to look after . . .) and all this had to be got through by 7.30; then

The Elizabethan kitchen at Canons Ashby with its huge cast iron Victorian range had to produce food for a large family, the house staff, guests and their servants and a regular flow of visiting tradesmen.

lay the hall breakfast, get it in, and clear up afterwards. Tea was provided at breakfast for the women servants and beer for the men. I was not rated as a man, but was allowed tea with the women servants, and was duly railed at by the other men ... My day's work followed on with cleaning knives, housekeeper's room, windows, and mirrors; lay up the servants' hall dinner; get it in and out and wash up the things, except dishes and plates; help to carry up the luncheon; wash-up in the pantry; carry up the dinner to the dining room and, when extra people dined, wait at table; lay up the servants' hall supper; clear it out and wash up. This brought bedtime after a day's work of sixteen hours.'

In spite of this rigorous schedule, William Lanceley appreciated the benefits his employment gave him, which may come as a surprise considering that he worked for four years before being offered a holiday. But his reaction to this apparent piece of good luck is instructive and revealing:' ... the family were paying a round of visits lasting six weeks and those servants who cared to take a holiday did so.

Very few did in those days and no servant would dream of asking for one unless the family were away from home. The butler and the housekeeper arranged the allotted time for each. My first holiday was three days, quite enough at the time. Our cottage homes and food were no comparison to what we had left behind.'

Sir Thomas Ingilby, who at the age of eighteen unexpectedly found himself custodian (with his mother) of Ripley Castle, for nearly 700 years the Ingilbys' family home a few miles north of Harrogate, has first-hand experience of service (as we shall discover later). His experience gained in what he terms 'the ultimate service industry' led to the publication in 2005 of his book *Yorkshire's Great Houses – Behind the Scenes*. In this he sums up the lot of the traditional servant in houses, such as his own, in one succinct paragraph: 'The relationship between owners and staff has changed beyond all recognition during the last four or five decades. If you were a member of the domestic household in the early 1900s, you had to be half-human, half-ghost. You lived a split-level life, spending daylight hours in subterranean kitchens, sculleries and pantries, and your nights in the attic rooms tucked away in the roof [which at Ripley Castle are used for storage these days]. Between the two, you had to be available but inconspicuous, silent unless addressed, ever attentive to the urgent summons of the servants' bells that lined the corridors. Free time was at a premium. The house became your very existence, and you relied on it to provide your wage and your social life.'

In 1925 Jenny Fowles began working as a scullery maid at Ripley Castle, joining the household of Sir Thomas's grandfather. Here she became one of a dozen domestic staff employed by Sir William Ingilby and his family, which amounted to a butler, two footmen, a hall boy (whose job it was to keep the cast iron wood-burning stove in the entrance hall stoked up and to take care of outdoor coats and umbrellas), an 'Odd Man', a housekeeper, cook, scullery maid, kitchen maid and three housemaids. In addition, Lady Alberta Ingilby employed a lady's maid, a Miss Stobbs. Jenny came under the supervision of the cook, Miss Patterson, for whom she prepared vegetables and sauces.

Attired as befitted her station, the scullery maid was
on the bottom rung of the hierarchy below stairs.

**Opportunities to escape from the regimented drudgery of life in service were few and far between.**

As well as the family, the kitchens fed the entire household staff; even so, all the ingredients were grown on the estate.

Jenny worked a standard fourteen and a half hours a day, from 7.30am to 10.00pm. She and the other domestic servants were entitled to one afternoon free a week, unless the housekeeper found extra work for them (which she frequently did). The servants at Ripley Castle were also allowed every other Sunday off. Jenny shared a bedroom in the Castle attics with another maid and in return for all this she was paid twenty pounds a year.

Her life in service brought its brighter moments, though. Lady Ingilby had a West Highland terrier, which was left with the housekeeper to be looked after whenever the family was away. However, the housekeeper was not particularly fond of dogs and passed the responsibility to the scullery maid. Far from resenting this additional burden, Jenny Fowles was delighted. Exercising Lady Ingilby's terrier allowed her to enjoy free access to areas of the gardens and grounds that the Castle's domestic staff were forbidden from entering without the housekeeper's express authority to do so. It wasn't only Jenny Fowles that benefited. On one occasion Lady Ingilby was so delighted by the appearance of her little dog when she returned home, that she rewarded the housekeeper with half-a-dozen silver spoons for having looked after it so well – not that the scullery maid was to benefit from her mistress's largesse. When Jenny Fowles left Ripley, it was to travel to Australia to work on a mission station: a month-long journey to the other side of the world that cost her five pounds.

By contrast Maud Barnes spent most of her life in and around the Cavendish family homes at Hardwick Hall and Chatsworth. Her father was Clerk of Works, first at Lismore in County Waterford before moving to Hardwick with his family in the 1920s. There they formed part of the small community that had grown up working on the estate for generations. School was two miles away and Maud and her five siblings walked there and back every day in all weathers; snow and torrential rain were no deterrent. 'Walking

home from school on the old lanes and up the park – you never met anybody,' Maud recalled. 'We would meet an old tramp sometimes, but no one would harm you.' The same freedom applied to holidays, when children of estate employees roamed more or less as they chose, spending all day away from home without their parents giving a second thought to their welfare.

As the youngest child, it fell to Maud to stay at home to care for her ailing parents after leaving

**Unlike the families that employed them, servants and their children had to go everywhere on foot whatever the season.**

33

school when she was fourteen; when her mother died in 1944, she looked after her father for a further fifteen years. That was the period when the then Dowager Duchess of Devonshire returned to live at Hardwick and opened the house to the public. Looking back at that time over fifty years later, Maud's affection for Hardwick Hall was as keen as it always had been. 'The dowager taught us about the house,' she explained. 'She loved it and loved to talk about it' – and in so doing equipped Maud to act as a guide to visitors, when she was able to find a few hours free from her duties as her father's housekeeper and nurse.

In getting to know Hardwick Hall, Maud turned her hand to a range of tasks, including darning frayed tapestries, which occupied her for hours on end. 'Since the National Trust took over [Hardwick Hall],' she reflected somewhat ruefully, 'they have had the money to send them away to be done professionally by the Royal School of Needlework, and when I go to Hardwick I think of all the raggedy ones that I was stitching away at.'

After her father retired in 1948, he and Maud moved to Heath, but her attachment to Hardwick Hall was undimmed. In her own words it was 'a very much loved house, especially by local people. I can meet people today who spent their young days in colliery villages around and about, and as soon as you say you used to live at Hardwick you're accepted.'

In 1959, the then Duke and Duchess of Devonshire moved into Chatsworth and Maud Barnes was asked if she would join the staff there: first as a housemaid taking care of the Duke and Duchess and then as Her Grace's housekeeper. This was the beginning of what the Dowager Duchess would later describe in her address at Maud's funeral in September 2000 as, 'so intimate a relationship for so many years'.

The sentiment was mutual. 'It was nothing like *Upstairs, Downstairs* with us because they were a youngish couple, you see,' Maud recorded in an interview in 1998 when she was eighty. 'There used to be a vast staff there, really. Before the war there used to be about 200 round about the laundry, kitchen, house, garden. When we went

**Chatsworth: the 'Palace of the Peaks'.**

**Phyllis Thompson, a long-serving member of the Harewood House staff, is a good example of an employee whose role has changed as visitors' needs superseded those of the Harewood family.**

back in 1959 the kitchen staff was four and a daily. She [Mrs Canning, the cook] was an old-fashioned cook who had been in service since she was fifteen and had worked her way up. When she retired they got young people from catering college and they have young people there now. And of course there are the modern means of cooking which we didn't have. Poor old Mrs Canning used to beat everything by hand, modern things were gimmicks to her – like making ice cream: there would be a chap winding this churn for hours on end.'

The Dowager Duchess's funeral address for Maud Barnes emphasises the important role Maud played during her days at Chatsworth. Revered by younger members of staff for the experience she had gained at Hardwick Hall of running a historic house, Maud was regarded as the last word on 'how a house like this should work and the various duties which have to be performed. "If in doubt, ask Maud" was the rule.' From helping Her Grace wrap her Christmas presents, to looking after family dogs as well as her own much-loved four-footed friends, to keeping a watchful eye on guests invited to charity coffee mornings, Maud Barnes personified what the current Duke of Devonshire defines as 'the incalculable value' of loyal and enthusiastic people working in historic houses such as his.

'If you built a house next door,' he suggests, 'you could do lots of things with visitor flows and have better facilities. But the one thing you absolutely could not replicate immediately would be loyalty [to the house]. You could get very nice staff, but they wouldn't have that loyalty to it.'

Part of that loyalty comes, understandably, from the relationship built up on a daily basis between owners and the people they employ. 'If you're around the house, or the garden,' the Duke of Devonshire explains, 'it's important not to be in too much of a hurry.' By his own admission, his wife is rather better at curbing the pace of her progress than he is, which gives members of staff the opportunity to stop her and mention something. 'If you're always walking fast, people won't stop you ... But if you're not in a hurry, they'll probably tell you something, which they'd be too polite to stop you for if they think you're in

a hurry to get somewhere. That is anecdotal and it's unscientific, but it's a very useful and interesting way of hearing things.'

It was at a staff training session, for example, that several guides commented to him on a change round of pictures. During the summer of 2006 a Rembrandt portrait normally hung along the visitor route 'in rather a key place' was on loan to an exhibition in Amsterdam. So a Reynolds portrait of Georgiana, wife of the fifth Duke, and her baby was hung in its place because it was the right shape and an attractive picture. However, as it was explained to the Duke, 'lots of people had missed the Rembrandt ... and I wouldn't have realised that if they hadn't told me.'

'People are absolutely the fundamental difference,' he readily admits. 'And we are incredibly fortunate to have that interest, loyalty and dedication.'

These days the 'front desk' at Chatsworth is genially manned by a team including Glyn Motley, formerly a gamekeeper on the estate and now one of the masters of the Lodge gates, who sees every kind of visitor: private, public and professional.

'He's pretty important,' the Duke of Devonshire points out. 'He has to deal with a lot of worried, lost, upset, frightened, cold, ill people because he is the first major port of call. So he is a key link – like the telephone people.'

By happy coincidence, more often than not, it is Glyn's wife Doreen whose voice you hear when you telephone the Chatsworth switchboard and, in the words of her employer, 'nothing is ever too much trouble for her'.

Fortunately, when it comes to employing helpful and sympathetic staff, it's quality, not quantity that matters. Roles may have changed, but it is the personal touch that visitors and clients remember. As its title suggests, Sir Thomas Ingilby's book reveals aspects of historic house life and work that might otherwise remain unnoticed. 'Stately homes have had to reinvent themselves,' he explains in his Introduction. 'In 1900 "a large household" would have been taken to mean a house with 100 or more staff, working in or in the environs of the house. By the end of the Second World War, that number would have fallen to perhaps twenty. Stately homes weren't the only traditional

employment sector to suffer a fearsome decline in employment numbers in the second half of the last century: farming, engineering and mining all went the same way. The extraordinary thing is that stately homes, which might at first sight appear to be the most traditional of those four industries, are the only ones which have actually recovered all of the lost ground: most of the those featured in this book employ just as many as, or even more than, they did a century ago.'

Unexpected as this may appear, the statistics speak for themselves. To quote Sir Thomas again, 'Harewood and Castle Howard, having slumped to a staff of twenty to thirty in the 1950s and 1960s, now employ more people than they did in the early 1900s. The Ripley Castle Estate employed seventeen people in the early 1970s, and many of those were part-time or seasonal jobs. We now employ over 100, and eighty of those are full-time employees; dozens more, working for local staffing agencies, are given regular employment here whenever we have a large event on. The story is much the same wherever you look. The renaissance has been so remarkable that

Yorkshire's stately homes now provide well-paid employment for over 2,000 people, and the graph is still rising each year.'

As in many other historic houses, people enjoy working at Ripley Castle or on the Ripley estate for long periods of their lives. The 2006 Yorkshire Show saw the presentation of long-service medals by the Yorkshire Agricultural Society to two Ripley employees, who had completed thirty-seven and thirty-eight years respectively in the same job; in one man's case it was the only place of employment he had ever known.

Working in a relatively small team in a historic environment with so much going on does call for flexibility on the part of everyone involved, owners included. There are few, if any jobs, at Ripley that Sir Thomas and Lady Emma haven't turned their hands to at some stage of building their business:

**Today's team at Ripley Castle reflects the change of working emphasis from family hospitality to commercial entertainment.**

9>39

cleaning loos, making beds, hoovering, doing overnight stints as night porter in Ripley's Boar's Head Hotel, serving in the Castle tea room.

'We do find that staff we've taken on for one job gravitate towards other jobs, sometimes quite dramatically,' Sir Thomas will tell you. 'We took on a cleaner in the late seventies, who brought her boyfriend with her. He started as a gardener. Then he came into the castle and was the first person to help me laying up tables … So he went on to manage events in the Castle for a number of years. And now he's gone outside again, because they're married with children, to work as Estate Foreman, carrying out all the maintenance and repairs in the deer park.

'What we've learned is that it's actually great fun to do another job. If the phone rings and there's a crisis at the hotel, various members of staff will leave the Castle and go and make beds. Or secretaries will help out in the gift shop. That's a bonus – doing something totally different to what you thought you'd be doing at the start of the day.'

Put simply, anyone happy to be as flexible as this must enjoy their work. Perhaps it is part of the process of establishing a close bond with houses like this; few who have stayed so long would deny that they get under your skin. Sir Brooke Boothby, whose family have lived in Fonmon Castle, near Barry in South Glamorgan, since the middle of the seventeenth century, recalls a touching instance of the kind of deep affection that houses such as his can engender in those who work in them. Years after retiring as head gardener, Mr Dobbs, as the young Brooke Boothby knew him, woke up one morning in his home in the village and must have had a premonition that he would be never be waking up again.

'So this very old man walked all the way up to the Castle, lay down in the garden and died. His relatives, who now live in Australia, come back every second year to visit the spot,' Sir Brooke says. 'And we have named a small border after him as Mr Dobbs' border. He hadn't been back for a year and a half. He didn't say a word to anybody. He just went there and that was where they found him.'

More recently a member of the Fonmon staff retired after sixty years of service; she actually began working at Fonmon in 1938, but specifically stayed until the millennium on the grounds that she had two years 'off' in the land army during the war. Her mother, long past retirement age, used to come up to the Castle to clean the silver twice a week; and she was still happily doing this when she was eighty years old.

In 2005 another employee at Fonmon retired after thirty years of service and at the party held to mark the event there were a dozen or so people in the room who had over 300 years' service between them.

That may well have been the case in other centuries. Samuel and Sarah Adams, servants with a wealth of experience of the late Georgian era, offered this advice to employers on the appropriate relationship to strike with their servants:

'In your manner to your servants, be firm, without being severe, and kind, without being familiar. Never converse familiarly with them, unless on business, or on some point connected with their

**From page to footman – eyes on the pecking order.**

improvement; but with this reserve, and distance of manner, be particularly careful to maintain kindness, gentleness, and respect for their feelings.

**If a housemaid was lucky, her mistress would follow advice to show her 'kindness, gentleness and respect'.**

Their patience is often unnecessarily exercised, and their tempers wantonly irritated. A lady, who filled every station of life with honour, both to her head and heart, attending the death-bed of an old domestic, who had been thirty years in her service—"How do you find yourself to-day, Mary?" said the mistress, taking hold of her withered hand. "Is that you, my *darling mistress*!" and a beam of joy overspread the old woman's face; "O, yes" she added, looking up, "it is you, my kind, my *mannerly* mistress!" The poor old creature said no more; but she had, by that last simple sentence, expressed volumes of panegyric on her amiable mistress. Human nature is the same in all stations; and if you strive to convince your servants that you have a generous and compassionate regard for their comfort, they will, in return, evince their gratitude …

'When servants are ill, their mistress will, doubtless, recollect that she is their patroness as well as their employer, and will not only remit their labour, but render them all the assistance of proper medicine, food, and comfort, in their power. Tender assiduity is half a cure; it is balsam to the mind, which has a powerful effect on the body, soothes the severest pains, and strengthens beyond the richest cordial. The poor dependent creatures may have no where to go, no one else to turn to; and their pale and impaired looks will always have a claim to your sympathy.'

Two centuries on, more people than ever earn their living in and around historic houses, in many cases filling a range of jobs that did not exist even fifty years ago. 'These are the new professionals,' as Sir Thomas Ingilby writes, and today those who own the houses and estates that employ them are as much professionals themselves in developing their various enterprises. Speaking as one who has learned his craft from the bottom up, he is eloquent in summing up 'service' today: ' . . . we serve the public when they come to us for a family day out, we serve the nation by preserving a quintessential part of its heritage, we serve previous generations by saving, restoring, completing and enhancing the buildings, gardens and landscapes that they have left us, and we endeavour to serve future generations by passing everything on in a better condition than we found it. We are not owners: we are custodians for the next generation.'

Service, it seems, is as much a family business as it always has been; the significant difference now is that the owning family is frequently far more serving than served.

# **Home** Produce

In the late nineteenth and early twentieth centuries many historic houses achieved a remarkable level of self-sufficiency, as illustrated by an anecdote told of Herbert Asquith during a weekend visit to Waddesdon, the Buckinghamshire home of the Rothschild family. Come teatime one afternoon, the prime minister was asked if he would care for some refreshment.

> 'Tea, coffee, or a peach from off the wall, sir?'
> the butler enquired.
> 'Tea, please,' Asquith answered.
> 'China, Indian, or Ceylon, sir?'
> 'China, please.'
> 'Lemon, milk, or cream, sir?'
> 'Milk, please.'
> 'Jersey, Hereford, or Shorthorn, sir?'

While not every household would aspire to such a comprehensive level of catering, it does indicate the degree to which large country houses had grown accustomed over the centuries to providing from their own resources much of what was needed, not only for the owning family but for their staff as well. When their numbers were swelled by the large retinues of visiting nobility, or even royalty, the catering requirements could be truly awesome.

In 1577 Queen Elizabeth spent three days at Lord North's house, in the course of which the assembled company ate prodigiously: '67 sheep and 34 pigs were consumed; 4 stags and 16 bucks were used to make 176 pasties; 1,200 chickens, 363 capons, 33 geese, 6 turkeys, 237 dozen pigeons and quantities of partridges, pheasants, snipe and all kinds of other birds, including gulls; a cartload and two horseloads of oysters, fish in endless variety, 2,500 eggs and 430 pounds of butter.'

The doocot (dove house) at Ballindalloch: illustrating that self-sufficiency in food, especially in winter, was a consideration in the design of historic houses.

**The team of garden and farm staff at any sizeable property complemented the ranking of domestic staff in the house.**

Self-sufficiency was a source of pride for many country house owners and the diarist John Evelyn made a point of recording a notable example, when he visited Sir Denzil Onslow at Purford, his home near Ripley, where he joined in a magnificent feast laid on for his host's neighbours. 'Much company,' Evelyn wrote, 'and such an extraordinary feast as I had hardly ever seen at any country gentleman's table. What made it more remarkable was that there was not anything save what the estate about it did afford: as venison, rabbits, hares, pheasants, partridges, quails, poultrie, all sortes of fowl in season from his owne decoy neere his house, and all sorts of fresh fish.'

In an age when beer was safer to drink than water, most sizeable establishments had their own brew-houses. Farm servants employed on home farms produced all the milk, cream, butter and cheese consumed in the household, while large kitchen gardens, often employing as many as a dozen gardeners, would maintain a year-round supply of fresh fruit, vegetables and cut flowers. This was no small undertaking, as one kitchen garden foreman complained to a newly-installed head gardener. 'There are so many departments,' he explained.

'There's the dining room, the steward's room, the housemaids, the pantry and the servants' hall, besides the kitchens. It's like feeding a factory.'

With so much produce available when it was ripe and ready to be gathered, and so many mouths still to be fed at times of the year when it was dormant or growing, a good part of the time of servants in many households was spent bottling and preserving garden produce, alongside other seasonal preparations. An indication of what this entailed was given by the inestimable Mrs Beeton in her *Book of Household Management*: 'In June and July gooseberries, currants, raspberries, strawberries and other summer fruits should be preserved, and jams and jellies made. In July too, the making of walnut ketchup should be attended to, as the green walnuts will be approaching perfection for this purpose. Mixed pickles may also now be made, and it will be found a good plan to have ready a jar of pickle-juice into which to put occasionally some young French beans or cauliflowers.

'In the early autumn plums of various kinds are to be bottled and preserved and jams and jellies made. A little later, tomato sauce, a most useful article to have by you, may be prepared; a supply of apples laid in, if you have a place to keep them, as also a few keeping pears and filberts. Endeavour to keep also a large vegetable marrow – it will be found delicious in the winter.

'In October and November it will be necessary to prepare for the cold weather, and get ready the winter clothing for the various members of the family. The white summer curtains will now be carefully put away, the fireplaces, grates and chimneys looked to, and the house put in a thorough state of repair, so that no "loose tile" may, at a future day, interfere with your comfort, and extract something considerable from your pocket.

'In December, the principal duty lies in preparing the creature comforts of those near and dear to us, so as to meet old Christmas with a happy face, a contended mind and a full larder; and in stoning the plums, washing the currants, cutting the citron, beating the eggs and mixing the pudding, a housewife is not unworthily greeting the general season of all good things.'

47

Before the days of refrigeration, preserving summer produce for winter consumption was a significant but vital responsibility for the housekeeper and her staff.

In large households the responsibilities of ensuring an adequate supply of all that was needed to feed, house and supply everyone with whatever their work required fell to the housekeeper, whose role was summed up by Sarah Adams, who had long experience of serving as a housekeeper in late Georgian England.

'The situation of a housekeeper, in almost every family, is of great importance,' she wrote. 'She superintends nearly the whole of the domestic establishment,—has generally the control and direction of the servants, particularly of the female servants—has the care of the household furniture and linen—of all the grocery—dried and other fruits, spices, condiments, soap, candles, and stores of all kinds, for culinary and other domestic uses. She makes all the pickles, preserves, and sometimes the best pastry.—She generally distils and prepares all the compound and simple waters, and spirits, essential and other oils, perfumery, cosmetics, and similar articles that are prepared at home, for domestic purposes. In short, she is the locum tenens, the Lady Bountiful, and the active representative of the mistress of the

family; and is expected to do, or to see done, everything that appertains to the good and orderly management of the household.

'She ought to be a steady middle-aged woman, of great experience in her profession, and a tolerable knowledge of the world.—In her conduct, she should be moral, exemplary, and assiduous, as the harmony, comfort, and economy of the family will greatly depend on her example . . .'

The sheer logistics of ensuring that the house was adequately stocked required remarkable powers of organsation and forward thinking. A glimpse inside a housekeeper's storeroom indicates the range of goods that had to be on hand in the days long before late-night shopping trips in the car to fetch last-minute items. Based on their experience in service, the authors of *The Complete Servant* offered this inventory and commentary of what a well-prepared housekeeper might reasonably be expected to have at her disposal for her employers and their servants.

'**SOAP** will be the better for keeping—indeed, it should not be used when newly made. The cakes should be cut with wire or string, into oblong squares, and laid up, on a dry shelf, a little distance apart, and across each other, so as to admit the air between them, to harden it.

**CANDLES** and **SOAP** made in cold weather, are best; and when the price of these articles is likely to be high, a reasonable stock of both should be laid in.

**STARCH** should be bought when flour is cheap, and may be kept in a dry warm place, if closely covered, as long as may be necessary.

**LOAF SUGARS** should be kept tied up in paper, and hung up in a dry place. Brown sugars should be kept covered up, and in a moderately dry place.

**SWEETMEATS**, **PRESERVES** &c. must be carefully kept from the air, and in a very dry place.

**TEAS**, **COFFEE**, **CHOCOLATE**, **DRIED FRUITS**, and generally, all kinds of grocery and condiments require to be kept dry and free from air.

The various kinds of **SEEDS** and **RICE**, **PEARL-BARLEY**, **OATMEAL**, &c. must be kept in a dry place, and be *covered close*, to preserve from insects.

**BREAD** is best kept in an earthenware pan with a cover.

**WRITING** and other **PAPERS**, that are constantly wanted, should be bought by the ream or bundle, and kept in a dry place.

**APPLES** should be spread, separately, on clean dry straw, on a dry upper floor, and care must be taken to preserve them from frost.

**PEARS** should be hung up, singly, by the stalk in a dry place.

**GRAPES** should be gathered before they are ripe, and may also be preserved hung up in single bunches in the same way.

**ORANGES** and **LEMONS**, if bought when cheapest, may be preserved a long time, packed in fine, dried sand, with their stems upwards, and kept from the influence of the air.

**FRESH MEAT**, **POULTRY**, **FISH**, &c. should be kept in a cool, airy place.

All salted and **DRIED MEATS**, hams, tongues, &c. should be tied up in strong paper, and must be kept in a cold, dry place.

**GREEN VEGETABLES** should be kept on a damp stone floor, and excluded from the air by a damp cloth thrown over them.

**CARROTS**, **PARSNIPS**, and **BEETROOTS**, must be kept in layers of dry sand for winter use. Neither these nor potatoes should be washed till wanted.

**POTATOES** must be carefully covered, to protect them from frost, in winter.

**ONIONS** should be tied in traces, and hung up in a cold dry place.'

Providing for oneself and one's household was not restricted to supplying the kitchen or the butler's pantry. In the limited amount of free time that servants were allowed to enjoy themselves, many employers saw to it that they were suitably occupied. The Reverend John Alington, owner of Letchworth Hall in Hertfordshire, was determined that his staff should improve their understanding of the wider world. To this end a large pool on the estate was converted into a scale model of the world. All the continents were represented and the Reverend Alington would be rowed around them by boatloads of servants while he delivered

**Abundant and varied produce from the kitchen garden was the pride of many a head gardener.**

lectures on geography. Back on dry land, these were supplemented by quizzes and discussions.

Not all employers adopted such an earnest approach to their servants' leisure time. In his memoirs, retired footman William Lancely noted the important part that music played in life below stairs. 'The Duchess of Connaught, who was very fond of music, encouraged her servants in this respect and a piano for their use was installed in the servants' hall. It was much appreciated and in a short time even the newcomers could play very well. A few took music lessons and these helped the others in their first attempts …

'There are always good singers to be found in large or small houses, and everyone knows that singing with music makes all the difference to a happy evening … I have often gone to the servants' hall to listen to a good song, and have been surprised at the talent that was under our own roof; two of the women servants were especially good and a footman and a steward's-room boy had both belonged to the choirs of two West End churches.'

**Estate community Christmas party at Chatsworth.**

Victorian Christmas festivities provided an opportunity for employers and servants to mingle socially. In the early 1900s the Duke and Duchess of Portland held an annual Twelfth Night servants' ball, to which 1,200 people were invited: house servants, estate workers, tenant farmers and local tradespeople. 'The rooms were beautifully decorated just as though the Duke and Duchess were giving a ball for themselves,' one Welbeck servant recorded. 'An orchestra from London was engaged and a swarm of fifty waiters arrived because none of us were required to perform any duties that evening – this was the social event of *our* season …

'It was quite a revelation to see all the members of the staff in ball dress. Even the prim head housemaid looked quite chic in a velvet gown, and the head housekeeper, who wore a low-cut satin gown, was almost unrecognisable … I found that we had acquired a new kind of individuality and gaiety for the evening and, stranger still, that we were all seeing each other from a new aspect – as people, not as servants.'

In the larger houses the occasional Servants' Ball gave the opportunity for the senior staff to emulate the manners and social ranking of their employers.

By the 1880s domestic technology had advanced to the point where country house owners who no longer wished to rely on oil lamps as the sole means of lighting their homes, and who could afford an alternative, had to balance the relative costs of building either a private gas works or an electricity power station for their own use.

In December 1880, Cragside, in Northumberland, became the first house in Britain to be lit by incandescent electric lamps in addition to being the first to be powered by a hydro-electric plant, as its Siemens generator could be conveniently driven by a small waterfall behind the house.

Two years later, the recently constructed Berechurch Hall, near Colchester, became the first house in Britain to be lit *throughout* by electricity. Its owner, Octavius Coope, had opted for electric lighting over gas lighting because electricity was much cheaper to produce privately than gas; his calculations showed that his new home could be lit with electricity for £200 a year, compared with the annual cost of gas lighting which would have been nearer £400.

While the high initial outlay of installing private power stations was the principal impediment to the widespread adoption of electric lighting in country houses, it was not the only objection. Many considered electric light 'insufferably vulgar', to quote Lord Ernest Hamilton, and it would take a couple of decades for it to become universally accepted.

Chatsworth had its own electricity supply from 1893, using water power to drive three turbines located underground in a building below the Emperor Fountain. George Maltby, whose father was house carpenter at the time, recalls being shown the turbine house in around 1923, when he was eleven years old: 'The first thing that struck me was the brightly lit interior and then the sparkle of polished brass dials and controls on the marble switch board and the hum of the turbines and dynamos …

'The speed of the turbines and therefore the electrical voltage was controlled by the water supplied to them [from the Emperor Lake over 380 feet above].

'The water supply was, in turn, controlled by a hand wheel and father said that when a house party was in progress, and a big chandelier was switched on, the house lights would dim but for the quick action of the turbine man, who would have to constantly observe the volt meter and rapidly change the water supply to the turbines to raise or lower their speed.

'The dynamos would charge a large lead acid battery set next door, which, in turn, supplied the current for the house.'

In 1936 Chatsworth was connected to the national grid and its power station fell into disuse for the next half-century. However, the alarming rise in electricity prices brought about a re-evaluation in the mid-1980s. Plans were drawn up by the assistant comptroller, John Oliver, to reinstate the turbine system and use the endlessly renewable, and free, supply of water to reduce electricity bills. The eleventh Duke saw the good sense of what was proposed and the same firm that had installed the original machinery almost a hundred years earlier supplied its modern equivalent. The process

The scale and demands of the largest stately homes and their desire for self-sufficiency justified investment even in miniature power stations like the hydro-electric plant at Chatsworth.

of repairing, reinstating and commissioning took eleven months. Then, ninety-eight years after Chatsworth was first lit by hydro-electric power, the new turbines purred into action on 12 December 1988, to do their bit in promoting renewable sources of energy – as well as cutting annual electricity bills for this historic house.

Four hundred miles north of the Peak District and Chatsworth, wind rather than water is providing the means to generate electricity for the scattered communities around the estate centred on Ballindalloch Castle: the enchanting Highland home of the Macpherson-Grant family, who have lived in it continuously since 1546. There was a time when wind and Highland castles, prone to draughty doors and windows and the chill of stone walls, with no heating apart from open fires, might have been considered uneasy bedfellows. Thanks, however, to more than forty years of loving refurbishment and careful planning by the present Laird of Ballindalloch, Mrs Clare Macpherson-Grant Russell, her parents and her husband Oliver, the castle is a model of comfort and warmth  – 'The Pearl of the North' – that

draws visitors to the intimacy and elegance of its delightful reception rooms and sumptuous bedrooms whatever the weather.

And what of the wind that buffets the surrounding hills above the Spey Valley? In recent years the turbines it powers have provided a revenue stream, index-linked for twenty-five years. This has established a known financial position for this particular enterprise among the mixture of activities that today make the Ballindalloch Estate viable, pays for the upkeep of the Castle, and secures this much-cherished family home for future generations. It's an ill wind, indeed, that blows nobody any good.

Mrs Macpherson-Grant Russell is another historic house owner who has turned her talents and expertise to writing; in her case the beautifully designed, top-selling and unashamedly enthusiastic recipe book "*I Love Food*". The title, and the author's opening injunction, 'Forget the battle of the bulge – indulge!' makes her book as tempting to read as it is to use – and this is due in large measure to the many recipes that draw on the abundant supply of fresh local game and meat

The agricultural emphasis varied from house to house – at Ballindalloch it led to the creation of the oldest herd of Aberdeen Angus cattle in the world.

that Ballindalloch has to offer its guests. Salmon caught on one of the estate beats (both the Rivers Spey and the Avon flow through it), pheasant, grouse and venison are all readily available during their respective seasons, as are locally distilled whisky to flavour sauces (and fortify the cook) and matchless Aberdeen Angus beef.

The Ballindalloch pedigree herd of Aberdeen Angus cattle was started by the present Laird's great-grandfather, Sir George Macpherson-Grant, in 1860 and is now the oldest herd in existence. The black cattle still graze peacefully in the 'Coo Haugh' at Ballindalloch beside the River Avon and

for more than a dozen years the Laird has shared a stock Aberdeen Angus bull with the estate of the late Queen Elizabeth the Queen Mother.

Few would deny that those dining at Ballindalloch benefit from these 'home' supplies of delicious ingredients, although one of those 'few' (during his childhood, it must be explained) was Edward Russell, the Laird's younger son. The story goes that he was away at a friend's house, tucking into roast lamb with more than boyish enthusiasm and complimenting his hostess on how good it tasted. Pleased as she was that he was enjoying her meal so much, she couldn't help expressing some surprise that he was not familiar with lamb at home. 'No,' her young guest replied, 'all we are ever given to eat is venison, pheasant, grouse or salmon.'

Home produce proved to be something of a mixed blessing at Ripley Castle as well. When Sir Thomas Ingilby's father was alive the home farm at Ripley still had a farm manager, half-a-dozen Jersey cows and three or four pigs, which were maintained solely for the Castle. Every day a churn of Jersey milk and Jersey butter fresh from the dairy would be delivered to the Castle kitchens. 'These were absolutely delicious,' Sir Thomas recalls, although their appeal waned somewhat after his father died. 'A new agent came in,' he explains, 'and determined that each pint of milk was probably costing us about eight pounds to produce, which was absolutely crazy. So, we were quickly buying our milk from the milkman like everybody else.'

(For a short time the gardeners at Ripley experimented with growing tobacco in the hot houses, along with more traditional produce like nectarines and peaches. It wasn't economics that put paid to that brief venture; it was taste. By all

accounts the Ripley tobacco was absolutely disgusting and, like the milk several generations later, the Castle opted to source its tobacco from more conventional suppliers.)

Jersey cattle have been supplying milk and other dairy products at Loseley Park since the herd was started by Michael More-Molyneux's grandfather in 1916, though the scale of production rapidly extended beyond supplying the immediate needs of the house and estate. By 1923 a retail milk round had been created delivering Certified Farm Bottled Jersey milk, cream and butter. In the words of his son, Major James More-Molyneux (Michael's father and author of *The Loseley Challenge*), 'It was top quality, top price and it made a small profit at a time when many milk producers were going bankrupt.'

In 1939 Michael's grandfather (a retired Brigadier-General) took to driving the delivery van himself 'by day or night, when it could be fitted in, dropping some crates of Jersey milk at Guildford Station to be railed to another dairy.' After the Second World War the Loseley retail business grew to around 500 gallons a day. Twenty years later the business had expanded to the point where Loseley Dairy Products were also producing top quality cream, cottage cheese, and yogurt, conveniently using old cow sheds and ancillary buildings adjacent to the house as their manufacturing hub – prior to that the cottage cheese, for one, genuinely lived up to its name – having been made in an estate cottage kitchen.

Ice cream followed soon after and with it the distinctive logo that established Loseley Dairy Products nationwide as the last word in top-of-the-range ice cream, yogurt and associated produce.

Here is Major More-Molyneux on how this came about: 'In those days, the 1970s and 1980s, the trend was for packaging to be very colourful. Daphne [the book-keeper/secretary/designer whose flair for business and marketing had first spotted the potential for cottage cheese production, from which the later products evolved] bucked this trend with clean white packaging, the House logo and LOSELEY in black, white and gold, elegantly projecting quality and purity. We printed Loseley House opening season and times on the pots and cartons below the House logo. With the

House open to the public, this helped to bring in more paying visitors and it stressed the point that our products are made on the Farm with the Elizabethan House which they could visit. In the surrounding parkland visitors could see the Jersey cows that produced the milk that went into the ice cream, yogurt and cheese and they could also go on a trailer ride to see the cows being milked. Apart from boosting our Leisure Department, it helped to build the reputation.'

That reputation has been sustained, although the More-Molyneux family no longer own the business, and the same quality standards that first established them with customers of Jackson's, Fortnum's, Harrods, British Airways and a large number of independent grocers, delicatessens and health food outlets continue to be maintained.

'Some children dream of becoming engine drivers, some firemen,' writes Major More-Molyneux. 'I had always wanted to a run a company.' When he was six years old he put 'Co. Ltd' after his name on the back of an old Wimbledon Tennis Tournament ticket, which he stuck to his bedroom door. During his schooldays he operated a series of business ventures among his fellow pupils, including a sweepstake and a

**Facing up to the post-war challenge at Loseley – the lady of the house mucking in.**

second-hand book dealership: both short-lived but satisfyingly profitable.

Although there may not have been any 'business' experience in recent generations at Loseley, looking back to the end of the eighteenth century Major More-Molyneux could draw inspiration from his ancestor Jane More-Molyneux. For twenty-six years her careful management of the estate and vigilant eye for the bottom line restored the financial viability of Loseley, which had been largely disregarded by her extravagant brother, Thomas, in the years before she took over.

Jane More-Molyneux kept meticulous accounts and instructions for running Loseley, which have been preserved and are now in the safe keeping of the Surrey History Centre. These reveal that her household, which included just nine servants, consumed five and a half pounds of soap every week for washing, cleaning and laundry, and that every month they drank their way through sixty-two gallons of ale and two large hogsheads [105 gallons] of house-brewed small beer. Her successor comments, 'There was no extravagance: at Christmas 1779 only half the mince pies were

1782.

April 9th Ann Huntington came here as Cook & Housekeeper at Twenty pounds a year Wages she is to have no Kitchen stuff nor perquisits of any kind.

Septemʳ 1ˢᵗ Elizabeth Stent came to me as Kitchen Maid — at five pounds a year Wages.

Septemʳ 7th Milley Caplen came to me as House Maid at Eight pounds a year Wages. — & five shillings a week board — Wages when I am absent from Losely — with a certain allowance of Coals & Soap — her Age 22. —

**Records of staff recruitment at eighteenth-century Loseley when a kitchen maid earned £5 a year.**

made before Christmas Day, because plums were so expensive that they waited until after Christmas Day "thinking the price might fall".

Examples from Jane's records cast a vivid light on the terms and conditions of employment Georgian servants could expect. On 9 April 1782, she noted, 'Ann Huntington came here as Cook & Housekeeper at twenty pounds a year wages. She is to have no kitchen staff nor perquisites of any kind.'

Five months later, on 7 September 1782, the accounts show that 'Milley Capler came to me as House Maid at eight pounds a year Wages & five shillings a week board – Wages when I am absent from Loseley – with a certain allowance of coals & soap.'

If this sounds parsimonious, a study of the scale of catering that Jane More-Molyneux provided indicates that her staff did not go hungry. An entry in the accounts headed '1781. April 20th: The Court dinner for the Manor of Loseley / held at Losely on this day. Memo.m: about thirty men dined here', prefaces a feast of gargantuan proportions.

The diners sat down to a table laden with:

Menu for the Court dinner at Loseley on 20 April 1781.

**First Course**

Calves Head Hash

Mutton Harrigo                    Roots
done savoury

Pease Soup

Roots                             A rich
                                  Rice Pudding
                                  Baked

Buttock of Beef

_____

**Second Course**

2 Roast Fowls

Hott                              Preserved
Apple Pye        melted butter    Orange
                                  sweetmeat

2 sweetbreads    Sallad           Six Pidgeons
Roasted          Dress'd          Roasted

                 mint sauce

asparagus                         4 Hott
                                  mince pyes

                 a Fore

                 Quarter

                 Of Grass Lamb

In addition, 'there was a Large Side Table on which was a boil'd Leg of Mutton & a very Large Plumb Pudding, w:ch took 2p:ds of Suet, & 2p:ds of Plumbs.'

An interesting sidelight is cast on the domestic arrangements at Loseley in another of Jane More-Molyneux's memos, which states, 'It is the custom here that all painters, glaziers & stone masons & joiners & upholsterers (when the family is at home) must eat and drink in the House: Breakfast & Dinner – when they are at work here.'

**Staff catering instruction from Jane More-Molyneux's housekeeping record.**

There is an understandable satisfaction that comes from providing much of your own food and drink. Although the brewhouse at Fonmon Castle had fallen into disuse by the time Sir Brooke Boothby's parents were running the estate, they were pretty much self-sufficient in food. Chickens, pigs, lamb and beef cattle were reared either at the Castle itself, or at the home farm. Potatoes were grown commercially in adjoining fields and the vegetable garden was as productive as it is today (when it not only supplies all the fruit and vegetables for Sir Brooke and his family, but also for the smaller functions of up to twenty people that take place in the Castle).

There was a shoot at Fonmon in those days as well, which came into its own unexpectedly at Christmas 1962, when snow began to fall on Boxing Day, heralding a period of near-Siberian weather that lasted for weeks. 'My two brothers-in-law, my father and I went out and shot food every day,' Sir Brooke explains. 'We were snowed up for ten days and we needed something to eat. We had a large house party, the place was full and whatever was in the freezer quickly ran out.'

There can be a downside to self-sufficiency, as an email from Sir Brooke in the summer of 2006 illustrates: 'Your letter arrived at a somewhat amusing moment exemplifying the struggle that it now is to maintain the old and the new side by side.

'On the public front, we have a wedding for 200 tomorrow, 100 for lunch on Sunday, then a "celebration of Welsh Women" on Monday, the WI on Tuesday, and someone's birthday dinner on Wednesday. Meanwhile it is my 30th wedding anniversary, my best man etc are arriving tomorrow, then we are all off to London on Sunday, giving a dinner party there Monday night then back to Fonmon Tuesday early as ITV Wales are filming the Castle and myself all day. So my wife wants the best orchids in London and the Head Gardener wants them here. The caterers want the main kitchen from 2pm tomorrow and I don't want to hustle my lunch guests. God knows which way the last asparagus will be split between the London and Welsh housekeepers as we traditionally stop picking on June 10th.

'All just about fine BUT we have lost the Welsh flag! Needless to say, tomorrow's wedding is one where they specifically asked for a Welsh flag to fly. So I have spent all evening hunting for a replacement – my cousins who have another castle up the road, can't find theirs either.'

A follow-on email a few days later reported: 'Flag found – folded neatly into a small Fortnum and Mason hamper and "parked" on top of the cache pot cupboard. So obvious; we just lacked the conscientious footman who would have remembered putting it there.'

Self-sufficiency in running a successful commercial enterprise in a historic house is all very well, but it does rely fundamentally on the 'self'. Once upon a time there were plenty of them and they were servants. These days, it can often be the owners and their families who are sent scurrying about to trouble-shoot the most recent crisis, hoping that the clients seated in the magnificent dining-room and tucking into delicious estate-grown fare remain cheerfully unaware that anything is amiss.

Staff sleeping quarters usually lacked privacy, warmth and comfort, although their employers often went without the 'luxuries' we take for granted.

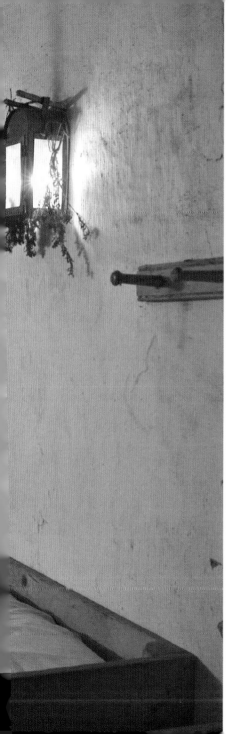

# Quarters
## & Catering

From the Middle Ages until well into the early twentieth century servants in many large households slept in dormitories that were very similar to the shared accommodation of soldiers and were also called barracks.

In the medieval period servants slept on pallets filled with straw, as described by William Harrison in the 1570s '…if they had any sheet above them it was well for seldom had they under their bodies to keep them from the pricking straws that ran oft through the canvas of the pallet and raised their hardened hides.'

Some members of the household slept in rooms close to their masters and mistresses, probably for security as much as convenience. Traditional four-poster beds that could be screened off by their curtains provided a degree of privacy as well as somewhere beneath which a servant's bed could be stored in the daytime.

From the late seventeenth century onwards servants' sleeping quarters were often located in the attic storey at the top of the house, partitioned into separate rooms or dormitories for half-a-dozen servants. Located right beneath the roof, these were often prone to extremes of temperature – bitterly cold in winter and stiflingly hot in summer – which must have made sleeping in them a trial. In some households a number of the male household staff were accommodated in the outhouses surrounding the stable yard, which on occasions reflected the dual nature of their work: with grooms and coachmen doubling up as footmen and not infrequently waiting at dinner and inevitably bringing the 'odour of the stable' with them.

A typical servants' hall where the off-duty lives of the household staff unfolded.

Servants in a medieval house would have eaten in the great hall, under the supervision of the house steward, though by the late seventeenth century dedicated servants' halls had come into being at the basement level of the house. Servants spent most of their daily life in the servants' hall, off which lay the butler's and housekeeper's rooms where the senior members of the household would retire. Just over a century ago the author of *The English House 1904–05* described a typical servants' hall as 'a large, long room; it must be as near the kitchen as possible but at the same time the butler and housekeeper must be able to keep an eye on it from their rooms. It is used not only as a dining room, but also a communal sitting room.'

It was in the servants' hall that visiting tradesmen might be received and where the visiting staff of house guests would be entertained. For the largest house parties additional butlers and footmen might be brought in to supplement the regular staff. With the servants of house guests further boosting numbers, it was quite possible for as many as one hundred people to assemble in the servants' hall on such occasions.

Samuel Nunney was a public driver in the Bakewell area when the horse and carriage still ruled the road and frequently conveyed the Duke of Devonshire and his guests when they needed to be taken to and fro around the countryside. Among his regular duties was helping to move the Devonshire household between the family homes at Chatsworth and Hardwick Hall. 'On the occasion of changing residence,' he wrote, 'it took as many as thirty vehicles of all kinds, from pair horse carriage to the three- or four-in-hand buses of those days, to convey the servants and luggage from Chatsworth to Hardwick, and the same on return. This was a great sight both for the townspeople [of Chesterfield] and also for those in the country along the route, and was also of great benefit to the business people.'

'I remember one occasion when King Edward [VII] and the Queen [Alexandra] visited Chatsworth there were over 200 servants in the house, including firemen, valets and maids of guests, who included the nobility of the country,' he recalled in his memoir *A Life on the Road*. 'One of the officials told me that he estimated that affair (a Ball) would cost the Duke somewhere about £30,000. As Chatsworth was an open house in those days we, as public drivers, had the privilege to enter the Servants' Hall, after seeing our horses stabled, and have served to you as much as you could eat and drink.'

This followed a pattern of catering above and below stairs that had prevailed for centuries. The Earl of Northumberland's Household Book, which regulated life in the early sixteenth-century establishment of the fifth Earl, details the domestic and social arrangements with military precision.

In addition to providing for his staff of 166, his household book specified the need to cater for fifty-seven strangers every day of the year. At the upper tiers of the domestic hierarchy his lordship was aided by a council of senior household officers, among them his chamberlain, controller, treasurer and secretary, clerks of the kitchen and of the signet, and a master of horse. They all belonged to the knight's table, which entitled each of them to three servants to take care of their daily requirements.

The regal nature of the Earl of Northumberland's home life extended to his public duties. Every Maundy Thursday he distributed Maundy offerings among the poor, just as his Sovereign did. In the Earl's case these comprised as many lined russet gowns, linen skirts, cups of wine and penny pieces as he counted years. His final act every year was to present the poorest man present with the gown of violet cloth lined with sheepskin that he wore on state occasions.

However, the cost of maintaining an establishment and lifestyle of this scale proved difficult to balance. Against an annual income of £2,300, his lordship's domestic outgoings amounted to £1,500, which left little to cover his time in London attending Parliament, travel abroad or even visits to other parts of the country. Such additional outgoings were not infrequently paid for with loans.

By the standards of just one generation later, savings were made on things like furniture. Only four of the eighty rooms of Leckonfield, the Northumberland home three miles from Beverley, were kept apart for use by the family. Even then they contained little more than trestle tables and wooden benches; decoration, such as it was, was reserved for the ceilings.

Aristocratic display, which in later centuries comprised domestic adornment, was concentrated in the Earl's household on clothes, even when setting out for war. In 1513 the Earl of Northumberland despatched 500 men to fight in France and each man embarked for Calais dressed in velvet and satin doublets embroidered with gold and silver. Every one of them took with him: twenty pairs of hose, twenty-five pairs of boots, twenty-one pairs of garters, fourteen hats and bonnets of various colours, a nightgown lined with fur, sixteen scarlet night bonnets and several suits of armour. Portable camp furniture and red leather saddles for their horses also formed part of the luggage train of this sartorially formidable force.

For all the finery and outer display down the centuries, kitchens and the equipment in them remained largely unaltered for hundreds of years. Well into the nineteenth century it was still customary to roast meat in front of an open fire on a spit, a skill that generations of cooks had mastered in line with principles such as these:

- 'Cleanliness must ever be the *maxim* for the kitchen.

- Before the spit is drawn from the meat, let it be wiped clean, and when done with, let it be rubbed with a little sand and water.

- A good brick fire, due time, proper distance, and frequent basting, are the chief points to be attended to in roasting.

- Beef and mutton lose about one-third in roasting.

- The ashes should be taken up, and the hearth made quite clean, before you begin to roast. If the fire requires to be stirred during the operation, the dripping-pan must be drawn back, so that then, and at all times, it may be kept clean from cinders and dust. Hot cinders, or live coals, dropping into the pan, make the dripping rank, and spoil for basting …

- It is as necessary to *roast slowly* as to *boil slowly*; and the *General Rule* is to *allow a full quarter of an hour to a pound for roasting* with a proper fire, under ordinary circumstances, and with frequent basting. But neither beef nor mutton require to be so well done as pork, lamb, and veal. Pork, in particular, requires to be thoroughly done. It must be basted with salt and water; and the skin or rind of the leg, loin, and spare-rib, must be scored, with a sharp knife, after it has been some time at the fire, to make it eat the better. Geese, pigs, and young pork, require a brisk fire, and should be turned quickly.

- Great care should be taken in spitting the meat, that the prime part of the joint be not injured: to balance it on the spit, cook-holds and loaded skewers are very handy.'

Even the great *chefs de cuisine* of previous centuries had to endure long hours in hellish kitchens to achieve their culinary masterpieces. Perhaps the most celebrated chef of the late eighteenth century was Marie Antoine Carême, author of *La Cuisine Française*, who served for a time as principal chef to the Prince Regent. A gourmet and a perfectionist, Carême would often begin working on a banquet at three o'clock in the morning, so that by the time the first course was ready to be served, he had been on his feet all day and half the night. On top of this he had to work in the conditions described here, all of which goes some way to explaining why he was dead before he turned fifty.

'Imagine yourself in a large kitchen at the moment of a great dinner,' he once wrote. 'See twenty chefs coming, going, moving with speed in this cauldron of heat, look at the mass of charcoal, a cubic meter for the cooking of entrées, and another mass on the ovens for the cooking of soups, sauces, ragouts, for frying and the water baths. Add to that a heap of burning wood in front of which four spits are turning, one of which bears a sirloin weighing forty-five to fifty pounds, the other fowl or game. In this furnace everyone moves with speed; not a sound is heard, only the chef has the right to speak and at the sound of his voice everyone obeys. Finally the last straw: for about half an hour all the windows are closed so that the air does not cool the dishes as they are being served, and in this way we spend the years of our lives. We must obey even when physical strength fails, but it is the burning charcoal that kills.'

If catering was hard for a master chef like Carême, it could be immeasurably worse for those lower down the pecking order. Employment as kitchen maid, or under cook, was how many young women began their work in service. The authors of *The Complete Servant* commented, 'This servant has, in many families, the hardest place in the

Watercolour of the main kitchen in the North Wing at Chatsworth, which was the hub of a series of rooms dedicated to various catering activities including a room for confectionery, a meat larder, a dairy, ice safe and plucking room.

house' – a statement that was more than confirmed by their description of what was expected of anyone engaged to serve in this position, in return for which they might expect to receive 'from 12 to 14 guineas per year'.

'It is her business, under the superintendence of the cook, to take nearly the whole management of roasting, boiling, and otherwise dressing all plain joints and dishes, and all the fish and vegetables. She is also, if there be no *scullion*, to keep the *kitchen*, *larder*, *scullery*, and the *kitchen utensils*, and every thing belonging to it perfectly clean, in the best possible condition, and always fit for use. On the due performance of this important part of her business mainly depends the credit

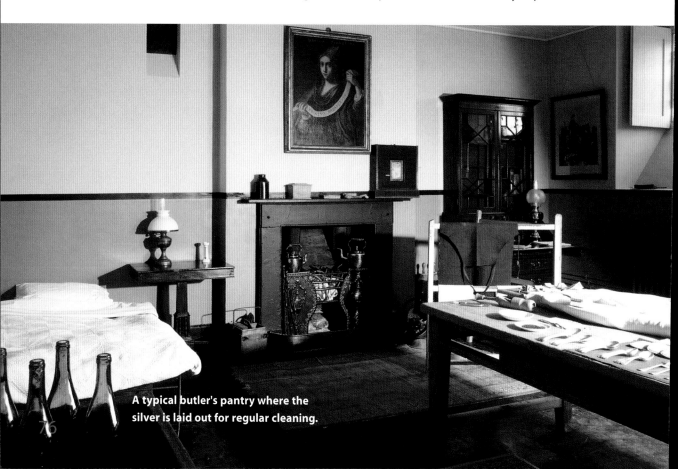

A typical butler's pantry where the silver is laid out for regular cleaning.

76

and character, not of herself only, but of the cook also; it therefore behoves the cook to see it properly done.

'The kitchen-maid must always rise betimes, light the kitchen fire, and set on water to be heated for all the purposes of the family, the first thing she does. She next scours the dressers and shelves, and the kitchen tables, with soap and sand, and hot water; and cleans up the kitchen; she then clears out and cleans the housekeeper's room, the hall and passages, the front door, and area steps, the larder, and the butler's pantry; in doing which, the scullion (if there be one kept) takes the dirtiest and most laborious part. She then prepares the breakfasts in the housekeeper's room, and the servants' hall. These things, if she be active, she will have accomplished before the cook begins to require her attention and attendance in the larder, in the furtherance of the culinary preparations; to which, however, she must have an eye, even from her earliest rising, particularly to the soups and other things, that require a long time to prepare.

'After breakfast, if not before, the cook will require her assistance in the larder, and afterwards for the remainder of the day she will be occupied in the kitchen, under the direction of the cook; first, in preparing for the servants' dinner, the dinner in the nursery, or elsewhere, and the lunch in the parlour; next in helping to get ready the family dinner; then in washing up and clearing away every thing, and cleaning up the kitchen; and lastly, in setting out and preparing the supper, either hot or cold, for the servants.'

Such was the situation in a Regency kitchen. Half a century later, Victorian kitchens had become cluttered with numerous gadgets, all of which required washing and cleaning by hand. The 1872 edition of *The Modern Householder* suggested this impressive list of kitchenware as being appropriate for a comparatively moderate sized kitchen:'… open range, fender, fire irons; a deal table, bracket of deal to be fastened to the wall, and let down when wanted; wooden chair; floor canvas; coarse canvas to lay before the fire when cooking; wooden tub for washing glass and china; large earthenware pan for washing plates; small zinc basin for washing hands; 2 washing-tubs; clothesline; clothes horse;

yellow bowl for mixing dough; wooden salt-box to hang up; small coffee mill; plate rack; knife-board; large brown earthenware pan for bread; small wooden flour kit; 3 flat irons, an Italian iron, and iron stand; old blanket for ironing on; 2 tin candlesticks, snuffers, extinguishers; 2 blacking brushes, 1 scrubbing brush; a carpet broom, a short-handled broom; cinder-shifter, dustpan, sieve, bucket; patent digester; tea kettle; toasting fork; bread grater; bottle jack (a screen can be made with the clothes-horse covered with sheets); set of skewers; meat chopper; block-tin butter saucepan; colander; 3 iron saucepans; 1 iron boiling pot; 1 fish kettle; 1 flour dredger; 1 frying pan; 1 hanging gridiron; salt and pepper boxes; rolling pin and pasteboard; 12 patty pans; 1 larger tin pan; pair of scales; baking dish.'

Within a hundred years the nature of catering in large country houses has changed dramatically. In place of significant numbers of servants who were employed, housed and fed in order to attend to the needs of the owning families and their guests, small teams of dedicated professionals have

**Families proud of their large staff would occasionally have them photographed and staff members would be given prints in which they also took great pride.**

established high-quality residential and catering businesses. The houses in which these are based remain as attractive and appealing as they always have – in fact the profits generated by these new enterprises are helping to restore and refurbish many historic houses which lacked the resources in the last fifty years or so that would have put them on a par with facilities provided in four- or five-star hotels.

The crucial difference is that historic houses are houses – not hotels. They remain family homes, with family photographs and family pictures on display (and occasionally family pets on lookout for titbits, or taking their ease oblivious to parties of curious onlookers). In more than a few instances the meals served to guests are prepared in the family's own kitchen and, in their start-up days, many historic house owners laid the tables, cooked the food, cleared away and washed up afterwards.

This was the early working pattern for Sir Thomas Ingilby and his wife among others – and they were clearly rather good at blending into the background. Lady Emma Ingilby achieved sufficient anonymity for one dinner guest to enquire confidentially of the attractive fair-haired waitress serving him, what is was like 'working for these Ingilby people?'

The pay wasn't that brilliant he was told, but at least she got to sleep with the owner. The weight of history in Ripley Castle and distant echoes of the feudal practice of *droit de seigneur*, that permitted a lord of the manor to bed every new bride married in his domain, quite possibly crowded in on him for the rest of the meal. And any lingering suspicions might well have been confirmed had he attended the function at Ripley when a heavily-pregnant

Lady Emma was on call to serve coffee to guests as they arrived in the morning. By the time they caught up with her again later in the day, she had nipped into hospital, given birth to the latest of her five children, and returned to be on duty when the guests reappeared for afternoon tea.

Mistaken identity can work the other way of course. An elderly spinster whose long-serving chauffeur had to be admitted to hospital for minor surgery went to visit him and was asked by the ward sister whether or not she was his wife. 'Certainly not,' answered the lady indignantly. 'I am his mistress.'

There is a magnificence, a grandeur, in historic houses and their settings that provide the perfect back drop for special events and one-off occasions, the most frequent of which are civil weddings and wedding receptions. But the portfolio of what takes place in stately homes that offer these services is wide-ranging.

Simon Foster is general manager at Eastnor Castle in Herefordshire, the dramatic Norman Revival house sitting in the foothills of the Malverns, which is home to James Hervey-Bathurst and his family. Simon and his team typify the kind of energetic, lateral-thinking event managers who are building successful and sustainable high-quality catering businesses in historic houses up and down the country.

Eastnor's handsome hospitality-cum-entertainment brochure, liberally illustrated with eye-catching photographs of baronial reception rooms and beautifully designed bedrooms of truly noble proportions and decor, informs readers that 'the Castle can be hired by business or private groups who are looking for an exclusive venue with a highly professional team on hand to help organise every aspect of their visit'. No doubt the same could be said of any number of commercial venues in the Welsh Marches. What gives the edge to Eastnor, and historic houses like it, is that clients have the exclusive use of a Castle that has hosted opulent, aristocratic gatherings for the best part of 200 years; that may, of necessity, reduce the number of functions that Eastnor can cater for, but it helps

to keep the special events held there 'special' in every sense of the word.

There is another important consideration in this strategy: the fact that Eastnor is a family home. 'If we were brutally commercial, we would just become a wedding venue,' Simon Foster explains. 'We probably wouldn't open to the public. We might not even cater for corporate events and just sell four or five weddings a week. But it would be absolutely impossible from every point of view. Most importantly for the family who live here; because the level of intrusion and disruption and the noise would be immense. The wear and tear on the house would be catastrophic. And I think the wear and tear on staff would be very difficult as well.'

Weddings, in fact, if they are well organised and run smoothly, are very hard work for everybody involved, very labour intensive and each requires a significant amount of administration. As Simon Foster puts it, 'If we had weddings every day, I don't think we'd keep our staff.' The fact that Eastnor, and every other venue offering a varied mix of business, do keep staff, shows the benefit of creating a stimulating working environment where people are happy to remain for years on end.

The commercial benefits are not limited to these venues. The design of many historic houses, such as Eastnor Castle, makes it impractical to cater for large-scale events 'in-house'. Instead, a well-established caterer in nearby Ledbury takes care of all the catering requirements; and her business is one of many located close by that appear on the Contacts List supplied to Eastnor's clients. From bands and beauty salons to stationery suppliers and string quartets, the majority have telephone numbers in the Malvern or Ledbury areas.

The design of the Castle makes it unsuitable for other types of function: for example, big conferences with several hundred delegates. Instead, Eastnor is being promoted as an exclusive venue for 'off-site business meetings and [small-scale] conferences', utilising the state rooms for presentations, product launches, seminars or boardroom meetings. The Great Hall, 'sixty feet high and decorated with works of art and suits of armour ... will seat up to 150 guests for theatre-style presentations'. Slightly over half that number can be accommodated in 'Pugin's lavishly decorated Gothic Drawing Room', while the delightful Octagon Saloon, overlooking the lake, 'is a perfect meeting room for boards of directors who are looking for complete privacy and beautiful surroundings'.

This particular room is a telling example of the direct benefit that stately homes are deriving from developing successful commercial enterprises based in the houses themselves, and it's an example that Simon Foster, for one, is genuinely thrilled with. 'Ten years ago the [original octagonal] carpet was threadbare: it had been there since the 1850s. So we commissioned somebody in London to have a new carpet made to match the original. It's a stunning piece of work and has transformed what had been a rather dull, shabby room.'

Eastnor has a long association with Land-Rover, which uses the 5,000-acre estate to test new models, teach people how to drive them off-road, and showcase the company's product range to key civilian and military clients from overseas. The fact that this can all take place in glorious

The replacement carpet in the Octagon Saloon at Eastnor Castle, like the ones in the Long and Little Libraries, was largely paid for by commercial enterprises.

countryside, with an 'Arthurian' castle nestling among trees close by – and available to the company for entertaining – has helped cement a business relationship that has served both parties well for over thirty years. It was at Eastnor, appropriately, that Sir Michael Edwards chaired the board meeting that set up Land-Rover as a commercial entity on its own, separate from the then British Leyland.

One of the attractive features of present-day hospitality businesses in historic houses is that no two are the same. They may have features in common, but each operates according to its particular circumstances and these, for the most part, are governed by the historic layout of the house itself. Eastnor Castle was built with a dozen bedrooms, in which guests can now be accommodated, whereas earlier castles such as Fonmon, Ripley and Powderham were constructed with other priorities in mind and simply do not have the space.

On the other hand, Ripley Castle offers clients a superb suite of rooms in the cleverly restored East Wing, where functions of every description can be

held – and this is in addition to the use of reception rooms in the Castle itself (medieval through to Georgian), that can cater for smaller groups. The same goes for Powderham, Fonmon and Eastnor, where guests can enjoy the grace and elegance of bygone eras, whether they are attending a corporate seminar or a sixtieth birthday party held in wonderful period reception rooms: libraries, drawing rooms, music rooms and dining rooms. This is definitely not a business in which 'one size fits all'.

Geographic location plays a key part in determining the kind of business that can be successfully operated – and when you are situated in a comparatively small sixteenth-century castle in the glorious, but fairly isolated, Highlands of Scotland, you have to develop a very different kind of hospitality business to those located within easy reach of millions of potential clients. This was the challenge that faced Clare Macpherson-Grant Russell, the twenty-second generation of her family to live in Ballindalloch Castle (and its first 'Lady Laird'), and her husband Oliver the best part of thirty years ago.

It would be easy to be starry-eyed about their home. Ballindalloch really could be modelled on a fairy-tale illustration – one of the promotional fliers describes it as 'The castle everyone would love to live in' and it unquestionably earns its billing as 'one of the most beautiful and romantic castles in Scotland'. Fond as they are of their home, however, the present owners have adopted a pragmatic approach to the upkeep and maintenance of both the Castle and the surrounding estate.

'Every Highland estate needs a banker,' quips the current Laird, although in her case the one she has in mind does not sit across a desk in a soulless office, but on the other side of the breakfast table. A banker by profession, Oliver Russell has provided the financial direction that has guided Ballindalloch since he and his wife took up residence in 1978.

Mrs Macpherson-Grant Russell will tell you that Ballindalloch is small and easy to live in. While that may be true, it is the fact that the *whole* castle is lived in *all the time* that lends it a particular charm and appeal. The drawing-room is used every day, and so are the dining-room and other reception rooms; upstairs guest bedrooms are regularly occupied. Family photographs are updated every year. The Laird's six dogs fly in and out, wherever they choose; one has a particular passion for television and can often be found at the beginning of the visitor tour watching an audio-visual loop that introduces the Castle to new arrivals.

This is what appeals to visitors touring the house and gardens, but it extends to house parties who come to Ballindalloch to enjoy its sporting pursuits: shooting, stalking, fishing and golf – and it was these that provided the incentive to start the hospitality business, prompted, as chance would have it, by a meeting of bankers.

**Present-day gamekeepers on the Ballindalloch Castle estate.**

Two weeks after moving into Ballindalloch, Oliver Russell was in London with a group of Scandinavian bankers, when it was suggested that they might have a management meeting in Ballindalloch, to combine their boardroom work with some fishing. Mr Russell takes up the story, 'So they came up and sat round the dining-room table for meetings in the morning and headed off to the river to fish, or enjoyed themselves on the estate in other ways during the rest of the day.'

'That started our corporate entertaining,' his wife continues, 'and really saved the whole estate. We had about a hundred properties and I've done up about sixty-five. We also had the shop and post office that had to be completely redone. We had a small hotel on the brae; that had to be completely done up as well. And it was all totally funded by our corporate entertaining, because at that time the estate had no money.

'In the old days, if my parents needed cash, they actually sold things. But Oliver, being a banker, was not keen about this at all. He said we needed to make money. But how do you make money with a few sheep? It was just impossible. So this is how we started' – and how her cookery book came about.

In those start-up days the Castle catering team comprised one housekeeper, who had been with the family for forty-eight years, and the Laird herself, plus a few people who came in to help in the evenings. The only snag with this arrangement was that the Laird had never had a cooking lesson in her life!

So she took herself off to Elgin Library, borrowed recipe book after recipe book, selected all the easiest recipes and made them even easier. As she disarmingly puts it, 'I had, not only to be hostess, but cook, bottle washer and everything else; it was quite a leaning curve.' 'Taste, Ease and Speed' soon became her culinary touchstones – as "*I Love Food*" bears out.

Fortunately, in recent years, the Laird has been able to share the kitchen work with a professional chef and the redoubtable Betty Cameron, who could well have retired by now if she wasn't indispensable (and the creator of quite delicious shortbread).

Simple servant's bedroom at Ballindalloch
Castle preserving its original austerity.

The bright, cheerful family kitchen in which they work may be a far cry from the Stygian horrors endured by Carême and cooks of the past, but Ballindalloch preserves one or two vestiges of its harsher history. On the way up the spiral stone steps of the circular Highland Tower, visitors can explore the bleak room that was once occupied by Castle servants. With stone walls and ceiling, and a flagstone floor, the winter temperature up there must have been numbing. The smell can't have been any more welcoming: the sixteenth-century privy set in an alcove comprises a hollow-seated stool, which would originally have stood above a pile of bracken or straw that was cleared away when the need arose.

There was another way of disposing of sewage in the Castle's earlier times: the corbelled Machicolation was a cunning device that enabled those inside to dump sewage (or stones, or any other projectiles) on unwanted visitors at the front door. With the development of the current highly successful hospitality business, it's fair to say that hasn't been used for quite a while.

**Mrs Betty Cameron – Ballindalloch's treasured family cook.**

# **Silver** Service

Until less than a hundred years ago, wining and dining in stately homes was almost exclusively the preserve of their owners and their guests. Larger gatherings for estate tenants and people living in the neighbourhood took place, of course, and were widely enjoyed. But the day-to-day round of offering and receiving hospitality in these great houses was limited to a select group of friends and associates, whose comfort and well-being was catered for by a sizeable household staff.

It has to be said that much hospitality provided in the great houses of days gone by was intended to impress (as of course were the houses themselves) and this was never more important than when royalty came calling. The enthusiasm for building memorable homes dates from the sixteenth century. William Harrison, the author of *Description of England*, looked about and concluded that 'never so much hath been spent in a hundred years before as it is in ten years of our time; for every man almost is his own builder and he that hath bought any small parcel of ground, be it never so little, will not be quiet till he have pulled down the old house (if any were there standing) and set up a new one after his own device.'

For much of that century, of course, advancement at court was closely linked to royal entertainment. Edward Seymour, Earl of Hertford, had to work hard to regain the favour of Queen Elizabeth I after his secret marriage to Lady Catherine Grey, sister of Lady Jane Grey and a potential rival to the Virgin Queen. He did this by investing in an unforgettable display of hospitality. Enlarging his own, somewhat modest, house for the royal visit,

Estate party at Eastnor marking the coronation of King George V illustrating that historic houses were often the focus of community-wide celebrations of national events.

he created additional halls, bowers and galleries and a royal withdrawing-room festooned with branches bearing bunches of ripe hazel nuts. Out in the grounds workmen set to excavating an enormous half-moon pond in which lay a 'ship isle' one hundred feet long by forty feet wide, from which sprouted three trees doubling as the ship's masts.

The Queen was met two miles from the house by a party of 300 wearing chains of gold and hats decorated with yellow and black feathers. On her way to the Earl's house, half-a-dozen maidens symbolically removed an obstacle placed in the Queen's way by Envy and her arrival was saluted by salvos fired from the ship isle. Emerging from a bower at the far end a 'pompous array of sea persons' waded breast-high to the Queen's feet. The entertainment continued with virgins on pinnacles serenading the royal guest with Scottish jigs. Silvanus, the ancient god of fields and cattle emerged in goat skins accompanied by followers dressed in leaves and was ducked by the sea god in the course of a water fight. After all this fun, the Queen was presented with a lavish gift of jewels

**The tradition of commemorative cakes (in this case of architectural subjects) continues down the centuries.**

before fireworks and a sumptuous dinner to which she was escorted by 100 torch bearers and 1,000 dishes. Sugar reproductions of all the royal castles and arms supplied a fitting dessert. It was a visit neither Her Majesty, nor her host, were likely to forget.

Extravagance in the dining-room could put a strain on family fortunes. James Hay, Earl of

Carlisle, was notable among Jacobean courtiers for his enthusiasm for culinary display. One sturgeon he imported from Russia was so large that special plates had to be made to carry it into the dining-room. He also introduced ante-suppers at court with 'dishes as high as a tall man could well reach, filled with choicest and dearest viands sea or land could afford; and all this once seeing and having feasted the eyes of the invited, was in a manner thrown away and fresh set on to the same height, having only this advantage of the other that it was hot.'

Hospitality of a different, though no less generous order, was a feature of Holkham Hall in Norfolk, home of Thomas Coke, first Earl of Leicester, which was celebrated for its sheep-shearing trials and the feasting that followed them. One guest, moved to record such a banquet in rhyming couplets, wrote of Holkham hospitality:

*They found thy viands good, thy draughts divine,*
*And much indulged in wit, but more in wine;*
*Deeply they drank who seldom drank before*
*And they who often drank, now drank the more*
*Then who can wonder of forbidden bliss*

*Should tempt e'en Whigs in such an hour as this?*
*Or what avails it now in rhyme to tell*
*How Anson strove to rise, but rising fell.*

The Earl was well known in America and American guests frequently attended the Holkham sheep-shearing trials, which evoked in at least one of them images of medieval pageantry. 'These shouts,' he wrote, referring to the Holkham toast – Coke's motto 'Live and let live' – 'echoing through the apartments of this stately mansion, standing alone in the midst of a rural domain and heard somewhat faintly in the statue gallery from the distant rooms, but still heard, had something in them to fill the fancy. The whole scene seemed to recall baronial days, the "moated ramparts, embattled towers and trophied halls." It brought back the remembrances of feudal banquets, as if here in alliance with modern freedom and refinements. So at least I felt.'

At the point of delivery, so to speak, for this kind of hospitality was the army of footmen employed to wait on employers and their guests. Almost entirely absent from great houses these days, the number and appearance (particularly the height) of footmen a family engaged were once yardsticks by which to judge a house and its owner.

The authors of *The Complete Servant* published in 1825 outlined what it took to be a footman of the first order: 'The business of the Footman is so multifarious and incessant, that in most families, if he be industrious, attentive, and disposed to make himself useful, he will find full employment in the affairs of the house, and the more useful he can make himself, in a general way, the more acceptable will be his services to the whole house, the greater will be his reward, and the more comfortable he will be himself.

'In many genteel small families, the footman is the only man servant, in which case he is expected to make himself generally useful; but his particular departments are, the cleaning of knives, shoes, plate, and furniture; answering the door, going on errands, waiting at table, and answering the parlour door bell. The footman finds himself merely in linen, stockings, shoes, and washing; but if silk stockings, or any extra articles are expected to be worn, they are found by the family. On quitting service, every livery servant is expected to leave behind him any livery had within six months; the last new livery is usually reserved for Sundays and dress occasions …

'In going out with the carriage, the footman should be dressed in his best livery, his shoes and

**The livery of a typical footman in the early twentieth century.**

stockings being very clean, and his hat, great coat, &c. being well brushed; nothing being so disgraceful as a slovenly exterior. He should be ready at receiving directions at the carriage door, and accurate in delivering them to the coachman, and though he may indicate the importance of his family by his style of knocking at a door, he ought to have some regard to the nerves of the family and the peace of the neighbourhood. When the carriage waits at routs or public places, he should abstain from drinking with other servants, and take care to be within call when wanted. His expertness in letting down the steps and putting them up again, and his caution in shutting the door, so as not to injure any one, or the dresses of the ladies are expected.

'When he walks out behind his mistress, he should preserve a modest demeanour, and protect her, if necessary, from intrusion or insult; and on this duty he is expected to be particularly attentive to every part of his dress. In answering the door it is his duty to behave respectfully to all enquirers after his master or mistress, and never to presume on his knowledge of persons whom they ought to see or ought not to see, except in obedience to positive instructions.'

This is what every would-be footman was meant to aspire to. In reality, his work could be rather different. William Tayler was employed as a footman during the early days of Queen Victoria's reign and kept a journal, which gives a first-hand account (in his own idiomatic spelling) of what it was like to work in service in this way. 'This is a very buisy day as we are going to have a party this evening something larger than usual. We had four to dinner and about fifty or sixty in the evening. The plan of manageing these parties are thus:– there are two men besides myself, one opened the door and let the Company in, I shewed them into a parlour where there were three maidservants to make tea and give it to them and take off their cloaks and bonnets, and the other man shewed them up into the drawingroom and gave in their names as lowd as he can bawl in the drawingroom. There is very good singing and music in their way. After they have been here some time, we carrey them up some refreshments on trays and hand about amongst them. This is all kinds of sweet cakes and biscuits, lemonade, ashet, negos, orangade and many other pleasent drinks but the best is the different kind of ices. This is stuf made of ice pounded, mixed with cream, and juce of strawberrey, some of apricot and oranges – in short, there are many different kinds. It's quite as cold as eating ice alone. It's eat out of glass sawsers with a spoon. It's from ten to sixteen shillings a quart, it depends on what fruit it's made of. The company comes jeneraly about ten or eleven o'clock and stays until one or two in the morning. Sweet hearting matches are often made up at these parties.'

Lady Violet Greville, social commentator and aspiring journalist, did not care for any kind of footman and submitted a withering article to the *National Review* in 1892, in which she railed against him for being ' … a functionary conventionally arrayed in plush breeches and silk stockings, with well developed calves and a supercilious expression. Several times a day he partakes freely of nourishing food, including a surprising quantity of beer. He has a wholesome contempt for poor people, small families, and genteel poverty; and talks of *us* and *we* in connection with his master. His meals and his pipe appear to be the be-all and end-all of existence. After comes the washing of his head. This has to done daily (so he avers) in order to prevent the powder he wears from injuring his luxuriant hair… He may be seen lounging superciliously on the door-steps of a summer afternoon, his coat thrown back, his thumbs in his waistcoat armholes, regarding the passing carriages and their well-dressed occupants with approval, or glaring contemptuously at the small boy with a parcel … He rises as late as possible; he exerts himself as little as he need; he declines to take up the governess's supper or to clean her boots … A jolly, lazy, magnificent fellow is the flunky.'

She would probably have been no more sympathetic had she known of the perils that stalked footmen when serving the great and the good at dinner. William Lanceley, who had years of experience in service, recorded two catastrophic episodes: 'The worst breakages that I remember were thirty-seven engraved and festooned

wine-glasses. The footman foolishly tried to open the pantry door still holding the tray.'

Then there was what he described in his journal as 'A sad accident [which] happened at a dinner-party when a footman was handing out two soups (a green pea and a clear soup); he was wearing an aiguillette [a cord, knotted at the shoulder] ... and the dining room chairs had a ball on either side of the top bar. The aiguillette cord caught the ball of the chair next to the lady he was serving and pulled him up sharp, the result was both soups were emptied into her lap. It was a pitiable position for both.'

Move the clock on a few years and Buckingham Palace becomes the setting for a similar catering catastrophe. Among the guests dining with the royal family on this particular occasion was the Canadian-born actress, Beatrice Lillie. Now the wife of Sir Robert Peel, she had made her name as an outstandingly successful comedienne in revues. Flamboyant and glamorous, she was wearing an exquisite evening gown when the flunky serving soup had the misfortune of unpending a ladleful into her lap. An awful silence settled around the table as he made desperate, yet decorous, attempts to mop up the mess. That was until Bea Lillie broke the hush and announced in ringing tones, 'Never darken my Dior again.'

Not everyone took a harsh view of footmen. Lady Diana Cooper remembered a very elderly footman at Belvoir Castle being excused the more strenuous duties given to younger men. Instead he was tasked with summoning the household at mealtimes, which she described as follows: 'He would walk down the interminable passages, his livery hanging a little loosely on his bent old bones, clutching his gong with one hand and with the other feebly brandishing the padded-knobbed stick with which he struck it. Every corridor had to be warned and the towers too, so I suppose he banged on and off for ten minutes, thrice daily.'

Lady Katherine Watney, sister to the present Earl of Devon, sheds a fascinating light on the transition in household service that took place in the middle of the twentieth century. With agriculture going through tough times, her mother hit on the idea of opening what amounted to a finishing school at Powderham Castle. Aside from hoping this would generate some income for the estate, Lady Devon shrewdly saw that young women brought up in households where servants had traditionally been employed would be facing a different way of life to that of their parents. Put bluntly, they were going to have to do things for themselves. The enterprise tailed off after five or six years, but in its early days twenty or so young women were domiciled at Powderham, receiving instruction from a number of experienced tutors. Someone came in to teach needlework. The pupils learnt how to do laundry. There were lessons in cookery. Lord Devon's butler taught them how to lay a table.

For the young Devon children, the presence of so many playmates was enormous fun. 'I remember we used to play sardines,' Lady Katherine recalls. 'Because they cleaned the house, they knew almost every corner of it.' Though not all, it would appear. 'I remember playing sardines on my brother's birthday,' she explains, 'and some of them got lost and quite spooked.' All of which is perfectly understandable had any of them looked for a hiding place beside Powderham's Haunted Landing, where the castle's 'grey lady' is prone to appear.

The resident ghost may still reside at Powderham, but the late Lady Devon's protégées are now, doubtless, running large houses of their own. The appearance and well-being of the rooms they cleaned and searched in games of sardines are now the responsibility of Ginny Bowman, who also works as the Castle's functions manager – a role that covers weddings, corporate events, charity balls, ride and drive days for car manufacturers and their potential customers, antique fairs, home & garden exhibitions, seminars, conferences ... the list goes on.

Twelve years earlier Ginny had applied to work two days a week as a guide at Powderham. These days she lives on the estate, as part of what she calls 'an extended family' and cheerfully admits to working 'twenty-four/seven' when the need arises. By 2004, the level of business she had built up called for extra help and now she and a small team supervise all the functions that take place.

The 1994 Marriage Act provided historic houses with a wonderful opportunity to develop new business. Many were already staging wedding receptions, but the new act made it possible for civil weddings to be conducted in premises licensed to hold marriages; the days of being restricted to the local register office had gone for ever. Today there are well over 2,000 licensed premises and the number is increasing, as is the workload for the registrars who officiate at civil ceremonies.

As a result many historic houses have become licensed for weddings, which now contribute a significant portion of the estate income. Seventy-five per cent of the weddings that take place at Powderham come from London and the majority of these come about through word of mouth. 'Our budget for advertising weddings is extremely limited,' Ginny says, although there is no shortage of couples wanting to be married, or hold their receptions, in the Castle. These can range from simple weekday weddings, lasting a couple of hours, to large-scale traditional ones, with an extensive wedding breakfast.

Although Powderham, like many historic houses, has its own chapel, this is not licensed for civil wedding ceremonies, which by law must be held somewhere without any religious associations or connotations. So, at Powderham, weddings can be held in four of the Castle's licensed rooms: the dining-hall, the wonderful Georgian music room, or one of the two libraries.

(Though even in a library difficulties can arise when applying for a wedding licence, as Sir Thomas Ingilby found at Ripley Castle. In every respect the library at Ripley has a dignity suitable for marriages; it's also large enough to seat up to seventy-five people comfortably. However, the presence of a picture – or more specifically, an item in a picture – caused one of many bureaucratic headaches that historic houses have to deal with. In this instance it was a portrait of Sir William Ingilby, holding what was just legible as a Bible, that caused the problem.

In order to receive his licence, Sir Thomas was told, the picture would have to be removed. The fact that it had been hanging there for three hundred years discouraged Sir William's descendant from shifting him elsewhere and leaving an awkward space in the room. Would it be better, Sir Thomas suggested, if he had the title of the book changed – to *Lady Chatterly's Lover*, perhaps? That seemed to settle the matter, and Sir William Ingilby continues to hang in the library at Ripley Castle while happy couples tie the knot beneath his benign gaze).

Back to Powderham – where clients who are holding a reception as well as a wedding can have use of all four reception rooms, in which case the wedding is held on a Saturday, when the Castle is closed to visitors. Depending on the number of catering staff brought in for the day, a wedding at Powderham can occupy the Castle with up to 200 people.

When it comes to coping with the unexpected and the unscheduled, Ginny and functions managers like her have to keep on their toes. One bride-to-be at Powderham suffered the horror of the zip in her bridal gown breaking as she was about to enter the wedding room. Fortunately she was wearing a full-length veil, which masked the

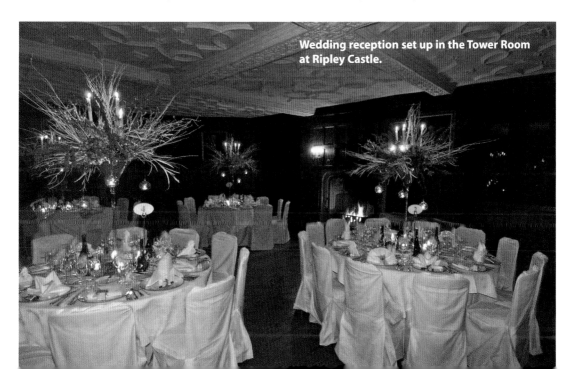

**Wedding reception set up in the Tower Room at Ripley Castle.**

safety pins that Ginny and a colleague had hastily applied to preserve her modesty as she made her way up and down the aisle. It was just as well that she and her husband had not been planning, as one couple did, a Morecambe and Wise skip back down the aisle after they were married.

Loseley Park typifies the approach that many historic houses have adopted to accommodate weddings: holding the civil service inside the house and catering for the reception nearby in the gardens. At Loseley small weddings are held in the Drawing Room, which is perfect for the intimate occasion, whilst the Great Hall provides a lavish setting for larger affairs. There is also the chapel at Loseley, which can be used for wedding blessings.

Fortunately the layout of these rooms means that there is not the disruption that can occur in other houses. At Loseley, moving a few pieces of antique furniture is all that is required to make the space for the forty or fifty gilt chairs that Michael More-Molyneux and a couple of helpers bring in at eight o'clock on the morning of a wedding when, in his words, 'we're all clean, and neat and tidy'.

In 1982 Michael's father had the foresight to reposition a seventeenth-century timber-frame tithe barn close to the house. Major More-Molyneux's idea was to use it as a shop and tea-room, little imagining that twenty-five years later it would the setting for wedding receptions catering for up to 400 people. With a dedicated firm of caterers on hand to take care of everything from a drinks party in the walled garden to a full wedding breakfast, much of the catering at Loseley leaves the main house largely undisturbed.

Michael accepts that he is lucky in this respect. In other houses the amount of furniture that has to be removed can be significantly greater, with the inevitable wear and tear that regular movement will have on any furniture, no matter how carefully it is handled, especially if it is several hundred years old. Even so, the amount of toing and froing at Loseley should not be underestimated. To illustrate this, Michael outlined the bookings straddling a weekend in July 2006. Starting on the Thursday afternoon there was a wedding reception, including a drinks party in the walled garden. This was

The Tithe Barn at Loseley Park.

The Library at Fonmon Castle.

followed by another reception the following day. On the Saturday, when the house is closed to the public, there was a civil wedding in the house requiring the furniture to be moved and the gilt chairs set in its place. Everything had to be put back on Saturday evening for the house to be ready to receive visitors on Sunday. Then there was another wedding in the house on the Monday afternoon, so out went the gilt chairs once again.

'Obviously there is wear and tear by the very fact that you are picking bits up and putting them down,' Michael accepts. 'If something gets scratched on a door everybody yelps, but I see it as a bit of a balance. It's no good saying that we mustn't do anything to disturb the dust; if we don't, we aren't going to get very far financially.'

He draws an interesting parallel between weddings and filming in the house, which can be a great deal more disruptive but does produce 'a lovely big slab of income when it comes in'. With the income from a day's filming equating to that from one wedding, it's clear that the upheaval caused by a week of filming is worth tolerating when it generates the same contribution to the bottom line as seven weddings day after day.

An example of the kind of precautions that need to be taken to protect delicate furniture comes from Fonmon Castle, where furniture is regularly on the move to accommodate various functions. Wear and tear 'is my greatest concern at the moment', says Sir Brooke Boothby. 'Down the back stairs, right next to the piece which is part of the old medieval staircase, there's actually an eighteenth-century Italian cabinet and an eighteenth-century clock as well, which are both totally out of place there – but they would not enjoy being moved. The net result was that I had to find somewhere that was dry, cool, where they would definitely not be moved.

'This is one of the hardest decisions, that I put quite high up the list,' he adds, 'how much I will allow furniture to be moved. You may not notice over five years; you may not notice over ten. But over a hundred years, I dread to think what may be happening – even with the best conservation going on in the interim … Once a piece reaches 250 years, you do have something of a moral obligation to keep it in good order.'

The dilemma he, and every other owner of a historic house, faces is that a hospitality business has to be flexible. Purpose built facilities in hotels, for example, are equipped with furniture that has a shelf life of twenty years, if that. Fonmon Castle, and many other houses like it, have that kind of utilitarian furniture too (in Fonmon it's stacked up, ready for use, in spare bedrooms). However, the appeal of using the facilities in their houses is that the rooms are decorated with beautiful period pieces. Remove them completely, and much of the charm of the house and its reception rooms goes with them.

This was precisely the predicament at Ripley Castle, where Sir Thomas and Lady Ingilby could see that their burgeoning business was also 'knocking seven bells' out of their beautiful historic home. To resolve this, they took the brave step of investing £3,500,000 in restoring the

The medieval part of Fonmon Castle provides an incongruous sanctuary from the hurley burley of weddings and corporate functions for precious items in the collection.

Castle's East Wing, which had formerly housed servant quarters and the stables, and converting it into a magnificent suite of function rooms.

By this time the Ingilbys were no strangers to catering, or to taking bold financial steps. After spending £1,500,000 on the Boar's Head Hotel in Ripley village, they opened the doors for business the very week that the recession started. When this was followed by the first Gulf War, the Boar's Head was, for a while, the most expensive and emptiest hotel in Britain. Their timing couldn't have been worse, Sir Thomas admits, 'We were a brand new hotel, trying to meet very good standards, but we had no track record; we had no established, returning clientele. It was very difficult. Other people had Lloyds; we had the Boar's Head – and the effects of the two weren't dissimilar.'

They almost left it too late to turn the business round, from which they learned a great deal, he acknowledges. 'With a huge payroll and no revenue, it was horrendous and we did have to sell an appreciable whack to pay for it.' Happily for them, their bank manager still had faith in the project and advised them to sell anything else apart from the hotel and the castle. 'This will become your cash cow,' he assured them, and a decade later he has been proved comprehensively right.

So much for the financial risks; the service side of the business had its roots back in the 1970s, when Sir Thomas's mother had run a tea-room in what had formerly been the outdoor servants' dining-room, serving cups of tea and making sandwiches for a couple of dozen people. After this she graduated to offering afternoon tea and occasionally dinner to visiting groups of Americans. However, it was the arrival of corporate clients that marked a step-change at Ripley. They wanted restaurant quality menus – and were prepared to pay for them. So the Ingilbys began hiring friends and neighbours who cooked, to come in on an ad hoc basis – some more successful than others.

'We had one cook,' Sir Thomas recalls, 'who used to believe in liberal alcoholic measures in both the sauces and himself. So it was a moot point whether the food would get out before the chef collapsed and it didn't always work out! It could be very

entertaining at times and he was a very inspired chef and did a tremendous amount for us.'

By this time Lady Ingilby had already followed her mother-in-law into the tea-rooms and, being a very keen cook, for a couple of years undertook the corporate hospitality cooking with a friend. Then an outside contractor, who had run a restaurant of his own, took over. With no permanent staff employed on the catering side at that time, help was brought in as and when it was needed to deal with parties of up to sixty-six in the Castle and several hundred in the almost permanent marquees pitched in the gardens.

At the same time Lady Ingilby had a growing family to care for and Sir Thomas an estate to run. So it wasn't uncommon for them to begin the working day at eight o'clock one morning and finally climb into bed at two or three the following morning – if it was a big charity ball, it could five or six.

'It was a very amateur arrangement,' says Sir Thomas. 'There wasn't a dishwasher in the place at that stage so everything had to be washed by hand, and if it was a do for five or six hundred people, as it often was, we would have to get three or four sinks in operation in different parts of the Castle and have different people hand-washing in each.'

Even when outside caterers were called in to help cater for the largest functions, the Ripley team, including Sir Thomas and his wife, provided basic staffing and wine waitering. Hands-on as they were, and invaluable as the experience was, Sir Thomas suggests that 'no one was as stupid as we were' not to get in more help to give them a bit of time off. He remembers that they attended a meeting held by the Historic Houses Association around this time. Fifty or sixty owners were there, among them a friend who told them, 'I give you four years to carry on as you are.'

'Almost four years to the day,' Sir Thomas says, 'we reached the watershed' and accepted that the business had to be put on a far more professional footing. Today Ripley Castle employs 125 people. There are ten professional chefs and four events managers, yet it still retains the feel of being very much a family business.

A quiet revolution was taking place. Magnificent country houses built to impress, influence and entertain were back in business (literally) after the decades of lying largely dormant. The Duke of Devonshire puts it likes this, 'For nearly a hundred years people didn't build big houses to show off … Hardwick [built by his ancestor the redoubtable Bess of Hardwick] is the easiest to understand. If you put your initials six feet high in stone around the top of it, you are not a shrinking violet. Bess of Hardwick has always been a celebrity, like Donald Trump. She was of the same mind; she was a dynasty person and she was very successful.'

The analogy he draws is telling and apposite. Commercial and economic power that was once vested in the builders of these great houses and their successors, now lies in City board rooms and on the trading floors of the world's stock exchanges. The need for display, for stylish entertainment, hasn't gone away, it's simply directed towards a new, and significantly larger, body of potential guests.

A few years ago these included delegations of officials and diplomats, headed by trade

ministers, attending a meeting of the World Trade Organization that was being hosted at Ripley Castle. Each delegation – from America, Canada, the European Union and Japan – was allocated a room in the Castle as their headquarters. Sixteen additional telephone lines had to be laid on, along with four photocopiers and fax machines. The Japanese minister, Mr Hashimoto, aroused particular interest as he was a front-runner in the forthcoming general election and stood a good chance of becoming the next Japanese prime minister. So ninety journalists flew in from Tokyo and overwhelmed the Majestic Hotel in Harrogate. 'The talks were fairly controversial,' Sir Thomas Ingilby writes, 'and for probably the only time in Ripley's history we received massive coverage in the *South China Daily* and on news channels like CNN.'

This was not the case in the local paper, however, which had been invited to attend along with everybody else. While the international media was focused on events unfolding a few miles up the road, it played safe and consigned coverage of the meeting of world leaders (minus a picture) to page five, where reports of other gatherings of local interest were printed: principally the WI reports. Meanwhile the front page was occupied by eye-catching items such as: 'Man exposes himself on Dallowgill' and 'Pateley man names chrysanthemum after former Knaresborough town crier'.

'When Sir Thomas Ingilby married Edeline Thweng in 1308,' writes his successor and namesake, 'he received Ripley Castle as a dowry. Wedding presents can be perplexing at the best of times, but it took us almost seven hundred years to work out what to do with this one!'

It may not be easy, and catering is a notoriously fickle business, but the Ingilbys, and the owners and staff building hospitality businesses in historic houses such as theirs, have every reason to be optimistic about the future.

# **Stables,** Laundries & Dairies

Most of us have become so used to jumping into a car to nip to the nearest supermarket, or receiving door-to-door deliveries of everything from milk to pizzas, not to mention the ease of loading our washing into a machine at home, that it's understandable if we overlook or disregard what had to be laid on in large households before these facilities existed.

Something else we take wholly for granted today is easy access to artificial light: flick a switch and any room is illuminated. As mentioned earlier, electricity in country houses is little more than a hundred years old. Until then oil lamps lit their interiors after dark and these required a lamp room, where the lamps were prepared before being put in place by servants. Delicate timing was required, as William Lanceley recalls from his days in service, when it was 'sharp work for the servants, who must not take the lamps in too early or leave the rooms in darkness'.

Inevitably the mix of combustible materials, naked flames and haste could lead to accidents, as was the case in one house that required the use of sixty oil lamps every night. Lanceley describes what happened: 'The footman had set light to all the lamps he required … and had used a wax taper for the purpose. He blew the taper out, as he thought, and put it down on the shelf. Either it was not quite out, or a draught caused it to flare up again; however it had been put near some waste that was used to wipe the oil from the lamps and this took fire in its oily condition, and soon the whole room was ablaze. A bracket just above the shelf, on which the lamp filler containing about a quart of oil was placed, was set on fire, and this in turn fell to the floor and carried the engine waste now burning furiously with it … The outbreak was discovered by the scullery maid. We had all been warned that in case of fire in the lamp-room we were not to throw water on it, sand only. The girl kept her presence of mind, called out "Fire", and ran for the coconut matting at the back door … The mat was wet and filled up the doorway, stopping the running oil; she then rushed to her scullery nearby, snatched two dinner plates from the rack and plunged them into a sack of sand which was used to clean pewter and copper utensils and threw the sand into the flames. The other servants followed her example and the fire was soon under control, but the smoke was dense and sickening. The footman, returning for more lamps, was dumbfounded … tying a lamp cloth over his mouth and nose he plunged into the burning room and brought out a four-gallon can of paraffin oil and a four-gallon can of colza oil. Had the paraffin oil exploded, another of the stately homes of England would undoubtedly have burned to the ground, as the nearest fire brigade was five miles away.'

Horses and carriages were to go the same way as oil lamps. It wasn't much more than a century ago that road transport of any kind depended on them. So country houses required stables and the larger the household, the larger the stables.

The same went for dealing with laundry. A household of several dozen required in-house laundry facilities on a semi-industrial scale, something similar to those found these days at large football clubs, where team strips from several sides have to be washed every Monday

**Typical dry-laundry room with stove for drying and airing laundry.**

morning. And in the best-regulated houses, Monday was washing day. In case any servants might feel tempted to put off the wash until later in the week, rhymes like this were posted in their quarters as a reminder of the consequences:

> They that wash on Monday
> Have all the week to dry.
> They that wash on Tuesday
> Are not so much awry.
> They that wash on Wednesday
> Are not so much to blame.
> They that wash on Thursday
> Wash for very shame.
> They that wash on Friday
> Wash in sorry need.
> They that wash on Saturday
> Are lazy sluts indeed.

Then there were the food preparation areas: pantries, still-rooms and dairies, where household produce was preserved and stored. The need for these has all but disappeared today. Fine wine may still gather dust and patiently mature in ancient cellars, but today's households no longer brew their own beer (or cider in apple-growing areas). Many historic houses retain their ancient brewhouse but they, and all these buildings, which were once essential to the running of a household, are now redundant.

Changes were afoot even ninety years ago. When Maud Barnes and her siblings moved to Hardwick Hall with their parents in 1925, they found themselves living in a house that had formerly been used for quite a different purpose. Old granaries, oast houses and laundries had all been converted to provide accommodation. With stone floors, large mullion windows and just a coal-fired kitchen range and open fires for warmth, the whole family suffered with heavy colds every winter.

When cars took over from horses, the buildings that had formerly housed grooms and other stable staff became available to other residents. Before moving into Powderham Castle itself in

**A very grand dairy (in this case at Blenheim) illustrating the range of customised rooms for various culinary and domestic activities of the household.**

115

1990, Lord and Lady Devon raised their family in the stables house down the drive, occupying space in this handsome building that had formerly been tack rooms for storing saddles and carriage equipment, with servants' quarters above; and as their family increased, Lord and Lady Devon converted more of the stables to house everyone. When they moved into the Castle, they swapped with Lord Devon's parents, who themselves moved down the drive to the stables.

Recent alterations have seen Powderham's former domestic wing, with the brewhouse and butler's pantry among others, rearranged to provide office space for the estate management team. This is still very much a working area of the Castle for the present generation of estate employees. Instead of washing clothes, brewing beer or making cheese, however, their work now involves managing the estate profitably and most importantly generating income from the wide variety of imaginative ventures which keep it going.

Like a lot of historic houses, Powderham has retained many of the original service rooms in the Castle, probably because there was never enough spare money to do anything else with them. The laundry now has a washing-machine, but apart from that, according to Lady Devon, it and the linen room are the same as they always were with 'the same paint on the cupboards apparently, the same shelves in the cupboards. Big sinks for washing the clothes.'

The former servants' hall looks as it always has too, although it is being used as a storeroom at the moment. However, its location close to the visitor entrance has inspired Clare Crawshaw, the general manager, with the idea of turning it into a study centre for educational parties. In the same way, the magnificent Victorian kitchen (doubling as another storeroom for the time being) is an unspoilt snapshot of where kitchen staff worked in days gone by.

Christine Manning has memories of this old kitchen when it was still in use, and of one member of the Powderham staff in particular who was closely linked with it. 'We used to have a lady called Elsie West, but she was always called Rary West for some reason. She was a charlady in those days . . . As a child, I remember being told that she

Early laundry aids still required a significant amount of elbow grease and effort.

The Victorian kitchen at Powderham Castle.

used to clean the old kitchen floor with a floor mop – and then mop the table with it afterwards!'

Rary West has long since passed on, but the heavy deal table with its three-inch thick top still stands four-square in the kitchen, piled high with bits and pieces that have nowhere else to go. But Clare Crawshaw has plans for this too. Once the clutter has been removed, she sees the Victorian kitchen and the scullery next to it forming another fascinating aspect of educational visits. Her aim is to present it pretty much as it was left, as if the cook, kitchen maids and scullery maids have taken a well-earned break and are due back shortly to start preparing the next meal. This is living history with a grimy face – and it's all the more realistic for that.

One of the ironies of many great houses is that they have very little space for storing things and here redundant rooms and buildings come into their own. Even a house the size of Chatsworth needs to use former servant accommodation for storage. At Eastnor Castle the stables provide convenient space. At Fonmon there are still horses in the stables, but they belong to people who work on the estate, not to the Boothby family.

Newby Hall, near Ripon in North Yorkshire, has a magnificent eighteenth-century stable block, with a classic quadrangle built around a cobbled yard approached through the impressive arch of a domed clock tower. Two hundred and fifty years ago, this was the communications hub of the estate – and it's still a communications hub today. In place of horses and carriages, the stables at Newby have been converted into state-of-the-art office space, fully equipped with twenty-first-century technology. Flexible, stylish and yet in the heart of gloriously tranquil countryside, the Newby stables serve as a fine example of how a redundant asset in a historic house has been turned into an income-producing centre that will contribute significantly to estate revenue for years to come.

Close by, at Ripley Castle, the challenge presented by the stables and adjoining domestic wing was even greater: quite apart from using them to make money, the entire East Wing was close to falling down. For Sir Thomas and Lady Ingilby, they always 'knew it was going to be the Sword of Damocles. It was the biggest single repair job that we faced – a seriously large one that was going to take more than the odd sale to deal with. We knew that the building was in an almost terminal state of repair and didn't have long left. And, as is the way with these things, no one could say you've got two-and-a-half years or fifteen years; it was an indeterminate date. We just knew that at some stage in the future that building would collapse – and it was moving.'

With only a limited amount of time available to restore it, the Ingilbys still had to be confident that the hospitality business they had built up was sufficiently robust to support the expenditure that was going to be needed for a job of this scale – and to keep the borrowings down to a level they knew they could afford.

In the initial meetings with their bank, Sir Thomas laid out the options they faced. They could spend a million pounds repairing, he explained, but all they would end up with would be the bare shell and the floors; they couldn't make a penny out of it because it still wouldn't be usable.

A major restoration and conversion of the stables and servants' quarters in the East Wing at Ripley Castle.

It was obvious that the bank wouldn't have been happy with that.

Then how about spending a million repairing it and then spending another two million pounds making something of it, Sir Thomas suggested.

This was also something of an alien concept, especially as the bank was being asked to undertake a significant capital outlay that would need a decade or two to pay back, never mind make a profit.

Sir Thomas tried the direct approach, asking pointedly, 'If you are our bank manager in twenty years' time, what do you want to see happening in this building?'

The reply he was given may have been unexpected, but it was very welcome, 'You're absolutely right. If I was your bank manager in twenty years' time, I would want to see that building used.' The challenge he faced was persuading the main board in London to sanction the somewhat unorthodox funding.

It took another six to nine months for the business plans to be worked up to the point where the loan was approved, but Sir Thomas is warm in his appreciation of the support that Ripley was given; it was a bold move on the part of the bank.

'You learn patience in this job,' he says with a wry smile. 'When you're working with old buildings, things don't get done overnight. It's a source of astonishment to people who are not used to doing it. They think you can apply for planning permission and start work in two months' time. But it's not going to happen. There will be delays, which will involve extra expenditure.'

The first year on the East Wing was spent working on the estate offices, which had to be moved out of the area they were about to convert. It was also important to maintain the appearance of the site, so that guests wouldn't be looking out from the

123

The Boar's Head Hotel in Ripley village,
providing a complete hospitality package
for Castle clients and visitors to the area.

Castle at a totally roofless building, which would have significantly spoiled what they were trying to achieve overall.

The second phase, lasting fifteen months, made the building structurally sound. Only after that could the actual conversion into a profit centre begin. In all, the building work took three and a half years, during which time the Ingilby family garden, out of sight of the Castle, disappeared under a builders' yard. 'It was the only place for it to go,' says Sir Thomas; for four years they and their children had nowhere private where they could sit outside.

English Heritage supported saving the building as one of the most complete stables and coach houses in the country. Having saved it, though, it was important that the conversion worked for the Castle business and furthermore appealed to its clients. Ninety per cent of the cost had to be borne by the estate and if the building did not become viable through the business the Ripley team were operating in it, it was clearly going to place the family and the estate at a huge financial risk.

The advantage of their years of operating even an 'amateurish' hospitality business, coupled with the challenges posed by the early days of the Boar's Head, made them realise the importance of flexibility. They didn't want to commit themselves to any single design or structure. Instead, they wanted buildings that were so adaptable that they could lend themselves to anything that was brought in to them, whether it was a corporate or a private function.

One of the factors that clinched whether or not they would embark on the conversion of the stable block was the volume of wedding business Ripley was having to turn away: before work even started there were over 1,000 enquiries a year. Once the new facilities were up and running three and a half years later, Sir Thomas and his team were able to treble the capacity of the business they had been doing until then.

Today slick Power Point presentations and the happy hubbub of contented diners have replaced the sounds of horses' shoes on flagstone floors and the ringing of bells in the servants' corridor summoning attention somewhere in the Castle.

But from the outside the restored East Wing looks no different to photographs of it taken when it was still in good order; for example in a *Country Life* feature dating from 1932. And this is exactly as it should be – the changes that matter lie inside.

Years ago Sir Thomas's father spent a weekend in 'one of Scotland's larger baronial castles'. The weather was wet, and in an attempt to keep his guests amused, their host had the inspired idea of using the servants' bells, each of which had a subtly distinct tone, to pass the afternoon. Guests were sent to all the rooms equipped with bell-pulls. Others were stationed at strategic points on staircases and corridors along the way, ready to convey messages from the Hall, where the owner of the castle directed operations. For the next three hours they tried to play 'God Save the King' on the servants' bells and failed lamentably. The din was so awful and the undertaking so pointless

that the servants escaped outside and left the house party to it.

That vignette encapsulates much of what has changed in 'stately service' in less than a hundred years. The servants' bells have fallen silent. In many historic houses the corridors in which they hung have been incorporated into redevelopments for other uses. House parties still enjoy happy weekends staying with friends in Britain's great country houses, but their comfort and pleasure is no longer the prime focus of the hospitality provided in many stately homes. Tens of thousands of guests, invited to a range of private and corporate functions, now enjoy the same elegant reception rooms and beautifully manicured grounds.

Visitors may have changed, but the sense of occasion, of enjoying something enduring and unique in a matchless setting, is as potent today as it was when guests arrived in horse-drawn carriages or chauffeur-driven Rolls-Royces.

## Illustration credits

Peter Wilkinson: cover, 43, 67

Britain on View.com
Martin Brent: 35
Ingrid Rasmussen: 51
Joanna Henderson: 8, 79, 83, 84, 104, 106, 108, 124

Oxfordshire County Council Photographic Archive: 10, 26, 46, 78, 115

Country Life Picture Library: 13, 27, 32

Mary Evans Picture Library: 15, 22, 23, 31, 41, 55

National Trust Picture Library: 18, 20, 48, 49, 52, 68, 70, 73, 76, 94, 96, 113, 114, 117, 127

Beryl Peters Collection: 24, 42

Felix Rosentiel's Widow and Son Ltd: 28

English Heritage/NMR: 33

Simon Miles Photography: 36, 92

Ripley Castle: 101, 121, 122, 123
Javan Liam: 39

Ballindalloch Castle: 45, 59, 86, 88, 89

Chatsworth © The Devonshire Collection, Chatsworth.
Reproduced by permission of the Chatsworth Settlement Trustees: 57, 75
Gary Rogers: 54

Loseley Park: 61, 62, 103

Documents from the Loseley archive on 63-65 (located at Surrey History Centre, Surrey County Council, 130 Goldworth Road, Woking GU21 6ND) reproduced by kind permission of Mr and Mrs Michael More-Molyneux.

Eastnor Castle: 91

Mainichi Press: 110

Powderham Castle: 118